ORIGINS

Volume 1
Bringing Words to Life

ORIGINS

Volume 1
Bringing Words to Life

by
Sandra R. Robinson

Teachers & Writers Collaborative
New York

Origins: Volume 1

"American Gothic (To Satch)" by Paul Vesey is reprinted here by permission of Samuel Allen.

Teachers & Writers is grateful to the following foundations and corporations for their support of our program: American Stock Exchange, Mr. Bingham's Trust for Charity, Columbia Committee for Community Service, Consolidated Edison, Aaron Diamond Foundation, Manufacturers Hanover Trust Company, Mobil Foundation, Morgan Stanley Foundation, New York Telephone, New York Times Company Foundation, Henry Nias Foundation, Helena Rubinstein Foundation, the Scherman Foundation, and the Steele-Reese Foundation. T&W also receives funds from the New York State Council on the Arts, the National Endowment for the Arts, and the New York Foundation for the Arts Artists-in-Residence Program, administered by the Foundation on behalf of the New York State Council on the Arts and in cooperation with the New York State Education Department with funds provided by the National Endowment for the Arts and the Council.

Teachers & Writers Collaborative
5 Union Square West
New York, N.Y. 10003

Library of Congress Cataloging-in-Publication Data

Robinson, Sandra R. (Sandra Rockwell), 1944-
        Origins: bringing words to life / by Sandra R. Robinson
    with Lindsay McAuliffe
        p.   c.m.
        Bibliography: p.
        ISBN 0-915924-90-0 (set) — ISBN 0-915924-91-9 (v. 1). —0-915924-92-7 (v. 2).
        1. English language—Etymology—Studying and teaching. 2.
English language—Studying and teaching. 3. Vocabulary—
Studying and teaching.
I. McAuliffe, Lindsay. II. Title.
PE 1576.R6 1989
422 .071´073—dc20   89-31355
                                                        CIP

Photographs: Sally Halvorson
Illustrations: Mary Azarian
Maps and word trees: Trevor Winkfield

Printed by Philmark Lithographics, New York, N.Y.

Table of Contents

Acknowledgments ix

Preface xiii

Introduction 1

Bringing Words to Life by Understanding How They Grow 5

Using *Origins*: The Teaching Materials in Volume 2 16

    Overview 16

    Introducing *Origins* 17

    Exploring Extended Meanings 27

    Reading Poetry 28

    Writing and Ideas for Other Activities 29

    Developing Your Own Word Families 34

    How Meanings Change over Time 36

    Exploring Popular Speech and Cross-Cultural Metaphors 38

    Sound and Meaning 41

    Sound and Spelling 43

A Brief History of the English Language 44

    The Anglo-Saxon Invasions 45

    Old Norse 48

    The Norman Conquest 50

    The Conquest Reshapes the Language 54

    The Renaissance 57

    English after the Renaissance 60

    The Mixed Heritage of English 61

    Indo-European Origins 69

    American English: The Story Continues 71

Linguistic Background 76

    Additional Word Families Based on Indo-European Roots 82

    Body Metaphors in English 92

    Exploring Popular Speech 94

    Sound Families 97

An Annotated Bibliographical Note 99

Appendix: The Words Project 103

    Using *Origins* as a Base for a Literacy Program 103

    Inventing Stone Age Languages 105

    Using *Origins* in French Class 105

    Exploring Cross-Cultural Metaphors 106

    A Final Word 106

Student Word Tree 108

Acknowledgments

Origins reflects the contributions of many individuals and organizations. I want to express particular thanks to those who played major roles in moving *Origins* from its tentative beginnings through to an active life in diverse classrooms and on to publication. The path was a long and winding one, and it seems remarkable, in retrospect, how the right people appeared at the right moment, by turns, to nurture, inspire, prod, push, and support the project.

When the first glimmers of *Origins* began to inspire my thinking, Bea Lindsten, head of the Potomac Middle School where I was teaching, offered generous encouragement. When I proposed teaching a new course based more on enthusiasm and ideas still bubbling to the surface than on any detailed curriculum, she responded with a sense of adventure. Her trust sustained my confidence and her office was a haven where I could share doubts, triumphs, and a love of language and history. Her whole-hearted support of my teaching experiments made the beginnings of *Origins* possible.

At the next stage of the project, David Hackett, then director of the Robert Kennedy Memorial, challenged me with a fellowship and a broader vision of the potential of *Origins* than I had initially conceived. From the moment I began talking with Dave about the material, he seized on its wide-ranging possibilities and pushed me to run with them. His support, through three years of fellowships from the Memorial and through major help with other fundraising, launched us (I was soon joined by my colleague, Lindsay McAuliffe) into piloting *Origins* in numerous classrooms in Washington, D.C., both in the inner city and in independent schools. His assistant, John Cheshire, instigated the Job Corps pilot, which further expanded our understanding of the possibilities of the material. Dave Hackett's challenge and support were catalysts that evoked many possibilities for *Origins* that would otherwise have lain dormant.

As I began to feel the need to write up new insights and ideas generated by four years of piloting a field edition of *Origins*, Jill Wilkinson appeared on the scene and offered support from the Stillwater Foundation. I am deeply grateful for Jill's patience, enthusiasm, and belief in *Origins*. She offered support for the final stage of writing this book at a time when we had no publisher in sight. I have greatly valued her personal support, as well as the financial support from Stillwater.

As I worked to prepare *Origins* for publication, Ron Padgett, my editor at Teachers & Writers Collaborative, and Christopher Edgar, editorial associate, made vital contributions to improving the clarity and organization of the text. I appreciate their help in pointing me toward revisions that were very much needed.

Calvert Watkins, editor of *The Dictionary of Indo-European Roots* (which is the source of the word families of Volume 2), provided an invaluable scholarly review of *Origins*, as well as its preface. He took time from a crowded schedule to go over two successive versions of the text and to help me clear up various points of confusion. I have appreciated both his help and the kind spirit in which he has offered it. Walt Wolfram, co-director of the Research Division of the Center of Applied Linguistics and professor at the University of the District of Columbia, also provided valuable advice and encouragement.

I would like to thank, as well, Sally Smith, head of the Washington Lab School, who had a major influence on my understanding of how children learn. Like my colleague and fellow author, Lindsay McAuliffe, I spent a year as an apprentice at the Lab School, where Sally trained us in using the arts and all the senses for learning. The Lab School overflowed with sculptors, dancers, musicians, and actors, and all of the artists and their arts were integrated into the teaching of spelling, math, reading, writing, and history. At the Lab School *kinesthetic* did not refer to the experience of moving a pencil across a page (touted by many workbooks as the "kinesthetic" element of an exercise); it meant that you got to your feet and *moved*. Being immersed in the Lab School for a year was formative. Many activities suggested in the word family chapters of *Origins* have their roots in that experience.

My collaboration with Lindsay McAuliffe had its beginnings in the Lab School connection. We shared a commitment to the kind of innovative teaching that had influenced both of us at the Lab School, and, when looking for a partner to help pursue the development of *Origins*, I turned to her. Her participation in *Origins*, from its early stages through toward its final form, has been invaluable. She took half-time leave from her teaching at the Sidwell Friends School and gave up summers to help write word family chapters, develop adaptations of the material required by the District of Columbia Public Schools, gather feedback from teachers who were piloting *Origins*, and prepare work-shops for teachers. I could not have shepherded *Origins* through its many incarnations without her help. The opportunity to spend uninterrupted summer days bouncing ideas back and forth between the two of us was particularly valuable to me, as was her expertise in running workshops for teachers.

As a result of Lindsay's work, other teachers at Sidwell Friends became actively involved in the development of *Origins*. Susanne Saunders broadened the scope of *Origins* and greatly enriched it by collecting poetry and developing writing ideas to accompany word families. Priscilla Alfandre generated great excitement among her students by having them speculate on the origins of words through inventing Stone Age languages. I would like to add a special thank you to Lisa Hirsh, friend and teacher extraordinaire, who spent a summer helping write materials for the word family chapters, and to Celia Alvaraz, my partner in the Job Corps project, who taught me a great deal about *Origins* as a resource for minority students through her own inimitable combination of generosity and unvarnished truth-telling. Her encouragement has meant a great deal to me. Eva Dömötör, partner in years of conversations that helped develop my teaching ideas, offered valuable insights. I would also like to thank Carol Kranowitz, Judith Steinberg, Bruce Boling, and Adrienne Carlee who provided important help and support along the way.

All the teachers who participated in piloting *Origins* played vital roles in its development as they plunged into using the material with their own students, posed questions and offered their own ideas. Working with the teachers who took part in the project was stimulating and a real privilege. Grateful thanks go to all of them: Vergaline Campbell, Doris Giles, McCoy Humes, Carol Robinson, and Yvonne Robinson in the District of Columbia Public Schools; Priscilla Alfandre, Michelle Jeffrey, Robert Peterson, Susanne Saunders, and Jennifer Swanson Voorhees at the Sidwell Friends School; Ann Craig, David Pines, and Ena-Mai Kvell at the Capitol Hill Day School; and Margaret Valiante at the Parkmont School. Carol Robinson provided invaluable help in adapting materials to the requirements of the D.C. schools. Cheri Bridgeforth, a doctoral student in linguistics, helped with interviewing teachers and gathering their ideas.

Lindsay McAuliffe and I are grateful to administrators at all of these schools for welcoming us. Particular thanks go to the District of Columbia Public Schools and the Sidwell Friends School for extensive help and in-kind contributions. We would especially like to thank Floretta McKenzie, Dr. William

Brown, Dr. Sheila Handy, Anabelle Strayhorn, and Leila Head of the D.C. schools, and Earl Harrison, Helen Colson, and Dr. Richard Lodish of Sidwell Friends for important administrative support for our work.

Gratitude is also due to writers and artists associated with Teachers & Writers Collaborative: Larry Fagin, Herbert Kohl, Bernadette Mayer, Jessica Sager, Daniel Sklar, and Felice Stadler.

Three artists have enhanced *Origins* by their contributions. Kate Rushin wrote the poems "Blues Song," "The Rapper as Light," and "Double Dutch Song" especially for *Origins*, contributions that have been favorites among students. Sally Halvorson made students' responses to *Origins* vivid through her photographs. Mary Azarian has captured a sense of the history that underlies English in her illustrations for the "Brief History of the English Language" chapter. We are honored to have these contributions.

The work that resulted in *Origins* would not have been possible without generous financial support from a variety of funders. In addition to major support from the Robert Kennedy Memorial and the Stillwater Foundation, the WORDS Project—the entity organized to receive funds and pursue the development of *Origins*—received major support from the Lyndhurst Foundation, the Cafritz Foundation, the Strong Foundation, and the Dreyfus Foundation. Additional support came from the April Trust, the Lucas Foundation, the Miller and Chevalier Charitable Foundation, the Riggs Bank, the Fairfax Hotel, PEPCO, the Chesapeake and Potomac Telephone Company, IBM, Hechinger's, Oliver T. Carr, and four individuals.

My own work in completing *Origins* would not have been possible without the patient and expert work of Judy Miller, who helped type the manuscript; the wonderfully reliable help of the young women who lived with us and helped care for my daughter—Rose Bailey, Fabienne Van der Keer, and Marty Cooper—and the support of my family. I would like to say a special thank you to Marty Cooper, who, with great patience and geniality, helped keep our household on an even keel during the pressured last months of completing the manuscript. The patience, good humor, and generous spirit of my husband David has undergirded my work on *Origins* at every step. I am deeply grateful for his belief in my work, which has never faltered over many years and many ups and downs, and for all his day-to-day help in freeing me to complete it. Finally, I would like to thank my daughter, Kate. The joy she brings to my life is an important source of energy in my work.

Preface

By Calvert Watkins
Department of Linguistics, Harvard University

Sandra Robinson begins *Origins* by emphasizing the role of verbal play in language: the creating of new combinations of words and forms and the stretching of expressions to apply to new situations. Likewise, initial language learning, which begins in the crib, is a very playful process. Children play-talk when by themselves, and they are well aware of this learning process. Many years ago my just-turned-four-year-old daughter and a friend of the same age were talking about—and illustrating—how they used to say words when they were "babies." The friend picked up her glass of milk and said, "I used to call it *mook*." Knowing her current pronunciation, I asked, "What do you call it now?" "Mook." "What's the difference?" With an air of complete self-possession, she replied, "Now I say it louder." If teachers can preserve, enhance, and foster that initial magical fascination with language, they will have accomplished their most enduring single task as educators.

Being creative with language is fun. What were the feelings of the first person to say *input-output*? Probably something akin to those of a precocious pre-school poet I knew, who on learning that a playmate's name was Ferdie, said, with a wicked gleam in his eye, "Ferdie-Berdie."

The particular creativity of American English shines forth in the words and phrases surveyed in the "Brief History of the English Language" chapter of *Origins*. A comparable list, equally poetic, picturesque, and exotic, could be drawn up for Australian English, as anyone who has tried to explain the lyrics to "Waltzing Matilda" will know. The same applies to all of the many other varieties of English, whether in Britain, Canada, Central America, Southern Africa, or the Indian sub-continent.

Being creative with language is not the only thing that is fun. Figuring things out is also fun. And knowing *why* can be very satisfying indeed.

There are a number of approaches to knowing *why* in human language. Some have to do with the psychological make-up of all human beings and seem to be characteristic features of most or all human languages: these are termed "language universals." In respect to such features, all languages are in some sense the same the world over. All languages have things like nouns and things like verbs. All languages have sentences, and these sentences have things like subjects and things like predicates. Most languages have in their lexicons forms like *boo-boo, cuckoo,* and *yum yum,* or expressive patterns like *wishy-washy* or *shilly-shally.* Studying and understanding such features (and others more complex) tells us something about the organization of the human mind.

But of course all languages are different, too, and the variety of languages is above all a product of language change. English is fortunate in having a fairly long period of documentation, and the history of the language, based on its written records, has been thoroughly studied and very well described. But historical linguistics—the scientific study of language change—is not limited to the study of written records. We know that English is not an isolate, but is closely related to other languages that make up the Germanic group, and this group in turn is one of the ten or so branches of the Indo-European family of languages. All these are descendants of a single prehistoric proto-language spoken perhaps some six or seven thousand years ago, termed Indo-European or Proto-Indo-European. The principal features of this language, its grammar and vocabulary, have been reconstructed by the techniques of historical linguistics.

The great originality of *Origins* lies in its utilization of both the documented history of English and of its reconstructed Indo-European prehistory as a touchstone to the teaching of language skills, particularly in elementary school. The method can work precisely because it evokes the spirit of verbal play, the magical pleasure in manipulating language. May *Origins* win new friends for the endlessly fascinating study of language, our language, and its roots.

Introduction

Beginnings and Development

Origins had its beginnings when a turn of fate led me to design a course on the history of the English language for a class of sixth graders. As I worked to gather materials that would inspire this energetic band of thirteen boys, I stumbled across the resource that gave rise to *Origins*—the "Indo-European Root Appendix" of the *American Heritage Dictionary*. The appendix revealed word families that appeal to students at an elementary level, families that reflected the poetry and playfulness of the language in particularly vivid ways. After a year of experimenting with ways of using the material and finding it did indeed seize the attention of the restless characters in my class, I knew I wanted to find ways of developing it for other teachers as well. When a request for support to run a summer workshop caused a year-long fellowship to fall into my lap, I was launched precipitously into trying an early version of *Origins* in two Washington, D.C., classrooms—one at the Brent School, a public school, and one at the Sidwell Friends School, a private school. Seeing students in these two very different settings respond with the same enthusiasm and lively participation to *Origins* classes presented by their own teachers confirmed my belief in the material. Students who felt hesitant in the world of books and writing felt at home with the get-on-your-feet, get-the-images-in-your-bones activities that introduced the word families; students adept at reading and writing responded creatively to the imagery and verbal playfulness reflected in the historical growth of the words. All were intrigued by seeing how the latest street language and popular speech spring from the images of our experience in the same way that words developed centuries ago.

Over the next several years, the project grew to include three third- and fourth-grade classrooms at the Sidwell Friends School; four upper-elementary classrooms in the District of Columbia Public Schools; three upper-elementary classrooms at Capitol Hill Day School, a Washington private school; a junior high class at the Parkmont School, an alternative school in D.C.; and a pilot literacy program for a class of Job Corps students, ages 19-21, who were reading at second- and third-grade levels. When Job Corps students took a lively interest

1

in exploring items of their own speech and then, in spite of initial aggressive indifference, started competing to be first on their feet to embody the images of a word family, I was once again convinced of the power of the material.

In all settings I—and Lindsay McAuliffe, who joined me in writing up materials—worked in partnership with teachers who were piloting *Origins*. We met to toss around ideas for presenting particular word families and then, after a class, to chat about what worked and what fell flat. The materials in Volume 2 of *Origins* reflect the play of ideas set loose as we worked together—both in pairs and in larger gatherings of all teachers who were working with the project. One of the many ideas that sprang from these gatherings—and was given shape by Susanne Saunders—was the formal inclusion of the poetry and of writing ideas that Lindsay and other teachers were already beginning to use as a natural outgrowth of exploring the word families. Later contributions to the poetry and writing ideas were made by writers-in-the-schools associated with Teachers & Writers Collaborative as they used *Origins* in New York City public schools.

Purpose

The purpose of *Origins* is to get students excited about language by tracing the histories of particular word families in ways that illuminate all vocabulary as well as important elements of reading and writing. The origin of a word has much in common with the origin of a poem or story. All have their beginnings in the stuff of our experience and take place through playful leaps of imagination. This broad understanding of word meaning animates all the word family chapters, as exploring the imagery of words flows into reading poetry and writing poems and stories. *Origins*, then, is a "vocabulary" book only in the broadest sense. We have found that its greatest value lies in fostering a delight in words. That delight has a solid foundation because, as students trace the development of word families, they acquire insights that help them understand all vocabulary in a more powerful way, habits of analysis important in reading, and resources for creating vivid language in their own writing.

Sources and Materials

The word families in Volume 2 of *Origins* came from Germanic and Indo-European roots. Drawn from *The American Heritage Dictionary of Indo-*

European Roots, the families have not previously been presented as teaching materials for students at elementary and junior high levels. We chose these families for many reasons: the vocabulary of the families is lively and down-to-earth and has great appeal for younger students; the vividness of the words makes them an inspiration and resource for writing; the abundance of words that have both a down-to-earth primary meaning and a secondary abstract meaning provides an excellent opportunity for exploring how abstract meanings develop. In addition, some of the families reveal ties of kinship between words of Germanic origin and words of Latin origin in ways that provide students with additional resources for detecting the many networks of relationship that permeate English vocabulary.

The scholarship that revealed the family ties in the word families we have chosen to explore was first made readily available to the general public in the "Indo-European Root Appendix" edited by Calvert Watkins and published in the 1969 edition of *The American Heritage Dictionary* (Boston: American Heritage Publishing Company and Houghton Mifflin). The Appendix was revised and updated by Watkins and published in 1985 as an individual volume, *The American Heritage Dictionary of Indo-European Roots* (Boston: Houghton Mifflin). If you check the Indo-European roots presented in *Origins* against this source, you will find a few minor changes were made. These were made in consultation with Calvert Watkins and are described in the "Linguistic Background" chapter. Examples of regional speech referred to in *Origins* are drawn from the following sources: *The Dictionary of American Regional English, Volume 1,* edited by Frederic G. Cassidy (Cambridge: Harvard University Press, 1985), *Maine Lingo* by John Gould (Camden, Maine: Down East Magazine, 1975) and *Down in the Holler: A Gallery of Ozark Folk Speech* by Vance Randolph and George P. Wilson (Norman: University of Oklahoma Press, 1953).

Structure

Volume 1 of *Origins* presents background material for the teacher. The materials include a general analysis of how meaning develops in words ("Bringing Words to Life by Understanding How They Grow") and a brief survey of the history that has shaped English vocabulary ("A Brief History of the English Language"). Although written for teachers, these materials can also be read by older students. The "Using *Origins*" chapter discusses ways of using *Origins* in the classroom and the "Linguistic Background" chapter presents a general discussion of the linguistic information found in the teaching materials.

Volume 2 presents teaching materials in chapters that explore individual word families. Ideas for exploring the families are presented in considerable detail in the beginning chapters in order to provide a full and lively sense of the possibilities that have emerged as students and teachers in many settings have used the material. Once students and teachers have explored a number of families, they begin to shape the material to their own needs and style, and therefore teaching ideas are presented in a more abbreviated form as the chapters progress. Most chapters include poetry and writing ideas, as well as ideas for exploring the word family.

How to Use This Book

For teachers who would like to get started using *Origins* without having to read the entire book, we suggest the following plan.

• In Volume 1: Read the "Bringing Words to Life" chapter. Then read pp. 16-28 and 38-40 of the "Using *Origins*" chapter.

• In Volume 2: Present the material in the BHEL, KER, GHEL, and WER families, and add the FLEU or DWO family, whichever is appropriate for your students. This plan works well as an introduction to the material. Later you can delve into other parts of the book and branch out to other word families.

Bringing Words to Life
by Understanding How They Grow

Who made up the words we use? How does language grow? How did the words *glint, glad,* and *glass* grow from the root GHEL ("to shine")? How did *rip off* and *spaced out* grow from the words *rip* and *space*? Language has always grown through the inventiveness of those who use it. Word families that developed hundreds of years ago and phrases of popular speech coined yesterday and today are the legacy of people who have been playful with root meanings, extending them to make new connections. The new connections—the new meanings—often reflect the experience of a particular time and culture. What is a "free-lance" artist? Standing in the historical shadows behind the free-lance artist or writer is the medieval knight who, rather than being attached to one particular lord, hired himself and his lance out to many different lords.

The teaching materials of *Origins* are designed to recapture a sense of the playful inventiveness that fuels the growth of language and a sense of how meaning is rooted in experience. Inventiveness is the lifeblood of all the ways we express ourselves in language—new words and phrases, poems, stories, plays. In *Origins,* exploring word histories spills over into reading poetry, writing poems and short plays, inventing new words—participating in the drama as well as reenacting it.

At the heart of *Origins* are the word families, which we explore with lots of up-on-your-feet, get-into-the-act, get-the-imagery-in-your-bones activities. We emphasize word families of Germanic origin because their words are often both colorful and down-to-earth. For example, from a root that means "to swell" we get the words *ball, balloon, belly, bulky, bulge, boulder, bold,* and *billow.* We also include families that, by going back to Indo-European roots, reveal relationships between familiar Germanic words and more abstract Latinate vocabulary. From the Indo-European root MEDHYO, for example, come the Germanic *middle, midst,* and *mid-* and the Latinate *medium, mediate, intermediate, Mediterranean, immediate, mediocre,* and *media.*

As we suggest ways to explore word families, our focus is on the images

5

and experience that underlie a word's "definition." In a typical lesson we might begin with a pantomime—of a wrestling match, for example. How do the wrestlers move? They twist or bend. *Wrestle* comes from the root WER, which means "to twist or bend." That image of twisting and bending was a resource for coining many other words, as well—*wrap, wreath, wriggle, wrinkle, wrist, writhe, wrong,* and *wrath.* Students examine the twisted strands of a wreath, wriggle into an imaginary pair of almost-outgrown pants, imagine the coziness of being wrapped in a blanket, writhe with pain after an imagined soccer injury, wrinkle their foreheads in surprise or in a frown. The root image springs to life in many forms, illuminating the words of the entire family.

Why search out the images that underlie *wrestle* or *wrap* or *wriggle*? Aren't the meanings of these everyday words easy enough to grasp without digging into their roots? The meanings of such words are indeed accessible. Many of these words, however, also leave their down-to-earth beginnings and journey forth to suggest abstract ideas. What do we mean when we say "Tony wrestled with the math problem" or "Demali wrestled with her conscience"? We wrap a child in a blanket, but we also wrap up a report and keep a secret under wraps—and become so wrapped up in the book we are reading that we forget to notice the time. We may watch a worm wriggle across a sidewalk, but we may also watch a politician wriggle out of campaign promises. The images we have explored as we first encountered the WER family become a resource for understanding these "extended" or abstract meanings. When Tony "wrestled with the math problem," did he get down on the floor and use his arms and legs to grapple with the problem? How is the *idea* of wrestling with a math problem related to the twisting, bending, and sweat of a physical wrestling match? Both involve struggle, both are difficult. When you wrestle with a problem in your head, you move back and forth in your mind, trying one thing and then another as you struggle to "get hold of" a solution—just as a wrestler moves one way, then another, trying to get hold of his opponent.

Tracing the evolution of the WER family words from their earliest roots to their latest abstractions dramatizes how we use our down-to-earth experience to express our flights of thought and imagination. Abstraction—literally "drawing away"—is one term that describes such evolution. Metaphor—literally "to carry beyond"—is another. Abstraction highlights the movement from experience to idea. Metaphor highlights the inventiveness that springs from our urge to coin new words and create new meanings. We tend to think of metaphor as an item of high culture. In truth, metaphor lives as vital a life on the streets and in the back hills, on farms and in computer rooms as it does in Shakespeare. It is a vehicle by which language—and indeed our very thinking—develops. *Chill out, bedcord strong,* and *he doesn't have both drives on line* are all as genuinely metaphorical as Shakespeare's "Sleep...balm of hurt minds." From the intuitive perception that our body temperature is lowered when we relax (*chill out*) to the experience of finding strong rope to hold the mattress of a homemade bed (*bedcord strong*); from frustration with the limits of a computer that lacks a second drive (*he doesn't have both drives on line*) to the experience of feeling balm heal a wound, the varieties of human experience are the clay we reach for to shape new meanings—or express old meanings in a fresh way. To express intangible feelings and ideas, we draw on what we know through the senses. Scenes from baseball and boxing become a resource for describing thoughts about somebody's conduct: *he's way off base*; *that's a low blow*. The unexpected twists of improvisation that occur as a jazz musician departs from the melody line to play "changes" become a resource for describing difficult times that put you through ups and downs: "Problems with her job have really been *putting her through changes*." An image of winds blowing "toward the harbor" is at the root of the word *opportunity*. The sensation of light and warmth suggested by the root idea "to shine" is at the base of a word that describes happiness: *glad*.

Exploring the word families of *Origins* provides a background for detecting the human experience and inventiveness that underlie the formal definitions of all words, whether they be words in the dictionary, the latest popular speech, or simply an unusual turn of phrase. Students studying the settling of the American West, for example, encountered the puzzling phrase "proving up on the homestead." What experiences on a homestead might lie behind the idea of "proving up"? The students had been immersed in *Origins* for several months, and the strategy of posing such a question was a familiar one. They were quick to come up with a list: clearing the land, building a house and barn, digging a well, planting crops. By the time they finished their list, they had a good sense of what the pioneers must have meant when they used the term "proving up."

Evoking the experience suggested by a root meaning provides a fuller understanding of how meaning develops than the unadorned this-comes-from-that approach. What, for example, is the meaning of the word *construct*? The root meaning of the word is to build (*struct*) together (*con-*). Why build *together*? If we simply set *together* beside *build*, its meaning may be puzzling, but if we delve into the experience it suggests, it can point us toward a vivid understanding of the word. What comes together in construction? A pile of logs, a stack of boards, a heap of stones or bricks. Or young saplings bent into a dome and covered by branches. Window frames, doors, plaster board. Water pipes, electric wires, insulation. Or chunks of ice carved for an Eskimo home. What holds these things together? Wooden pegs, animal sinew, nails, cement. By the time we have explored the experience suggested by the *con-* of *construct* (in conjunction with our understanding of *build*), we have a full-bodied sense of the word.

The same approach—What is the experience at the root of this word?—can illuminate the multiple meanings of a word. In *The American Heritage Dictionary*, for example, more than thirty-five meanings are given for the word *draw*. Such a long list of meanings can be daunting. The list becomes manageable, however, if we see the many meanings not as separate and discrete, but as a family of related meanings that have grown from the experience of *pulling* that lies at the root of the word—an experience we can discover in its primary meaning. A chimney that *draws* well is one whose air currents *pull* smoke upward; the concept of money *drawing* interest is a metaphorical *pulling* of one thing toward another; someone who *draws* a picture *pulls* a pen or pencil across a surface; and a fiction writer who *draws* a scene in a novel does so by a metaphorical extension of an artist's drawing.

The *Origins* angle of vision on language also provides a foundation for valuing students' own speech. Whatever background and interests students may have, their conversation will include lively figures of speech that reflect the kind of inventive thinking that has fueled the growth of language throughout history. From the latest popular speech to the vocabulary of a non-standard dialect or the vocabulary of strikingly different languages such as Chinese or Arabic, there are words and expressions in a student's own language that can be illuminated by delving into the experience that underlies their meaning. Exploring such expressions often generates an enthusiasm that then carries over into exploring the word families. When students feel they are part of the story, they are more interested in studying it. The "Using *Origins*" chapter provides additional thoughts on digging into the roots of popular speech.

Even when students' home language is wholly unrelated to English, exploring metaphors based on shared experience can establish a sense of connection between the language of home and school. In all languages, vocabulary is rooted in experience, and basic to all of us, whatever language we speak, is that we experience the world through our bodies. In English, many metaphors are rooted in this experience of the body. We may aspire to be *head* of a company, our achievements may inspire us to hold our *heads* high, we may be *head*strong in pursuit of what we want, or we may take on more than we can *handle* and find ourselves in over our *heads*. A person who is deceitful may be described as two-*faced*. We may be *nosy*, we may *nose* into a parking space, or we may look down our *noses* at others. If we want to ignore something, we may turn a blind *eye* to it—or turn a deaf *ear* to it. On the other hand, we may lend an *ear*—or even be all *ears*. You can be firm and put your *foot* down—or you can throw up your *hands* and give in. You may *shoulder* a burden or get cold *feet* and avoid it. A person may be cold-*hearted* or warm-*hearted*, hard-*hearted* or soft-*hearted*—or *heartless*. We can take *heart* or lose *heart*—and we can attack a job half-*heartedly* or whole-*heartedly*. Any group that sits down to brainstorm such a list will come up with many other examples. Such examples provide a jumping off point for eliciting similar metaphors in other languages. So far, all the languages we've investigated have yielded such expressions. In Arabic, the word for the *head of a company* or *head of state* is also built on the Arabic word for *head*—and the same is true in Thai. In Hungarian, the word for disorder or anarchy is "headlessness." In Hebrew, Rosh Hashanah means "head of the year." In Tagalog, a language of the Philippines, the word for generous means, literally, "with open palm." In Temne, one of the languages of Sierra Leone, having a "good hand" means, figuratively, that everything you do turns out well. In Wolof, an African language, to have a "clean heart" is to be sincere.

Exploring students' own speech helps to awaken the sense fostered by all of the *Origins* material—that the story of how language grows belongs to us all. A group of reluctant Job Corps students became interested in spite of themselves when we started exploring word origins by examining items in their own speech. Nineteen- to twenty-one-year-olds who were reading at second- and third-grade levels, these students were hardly eager learners. By the end of a week, however, they were claiming the first word family as their own and competing to be first on their feet to dramatize a word. They developed a grudging admiration for those people of the past who, by coining the words of the BHEL family, knew how to be as slick with words as they were.

We have found that the *Origins* approach to exploring word families and students' own speech sparks a delight in words and illuminates many corners of the language arts curriculum. "That's one of our words!" echoes through classrooms where students have been tracing the life history of *Origins* vocabulary. In one inner-city class, virtually the entire group turned to their teacher, whispering and smiling with recognition as a *duet* (a member of the DWO family they were studying) was announced in assembly. Most important, the sense of family feeling developed for the particular vocabulary of *Origins* begins to spread to words in general. Where do they come from? What are their relatives? "I bet *handle* comes from *hand*, right?" "Hey, *split* is like *rip off*. When you split, you separate yourself—you get going away from where you've been." "*Nestle* must be related to *nest*! If you're going to nestle down in something, it's like getting in your nest." Everyday words take on new life. Unfamiliar words kindle new interest. Where do they come from? Do they have any word cousins? Students who have been immersed in *Origins* are eager to hear such stories—and teachers who have been using the material are alert to the pleasures of finding and telling them. When a third grader was puzzled by the meaning of the word *cardiac*, encountered in a book she was reading, her teacher not only helped her discover the root meaning of the word ("heart") but also introduced her to two other members of the family—*courage* and *accord*. How might *courage* and *cardiac* be related? "Because you have to have a big *heart* to be courageous," came the immediate reply. And *accord*? Together they explored its meaning as a "meeting of hearts." Because exploring *Origins* word families—including reasons for frequent vowel shifts within a root pattern (*car-, cour-, cor-*)—had been so much a part of the classroom experience, the discussion took only a moment. The territory was familiar. Several days later the third grader referred, with a smile, to her "heart" family.

Delight in words begins to animate students' writing, as well. The lively vocabulary of *Origins* word families shows up with growing frequency in

stories and poems. The images and words of a family can also be a formal inspiration for writing. A brainstorming meditation on *gold* (another member of the GHEL family), launched a writing session for a class of Washington, D.C., fourth graders. Here is one of their poems:

Gold

Gold,
    its reflection bends
    the earth
        with awe.
It tempts
     the gangsters
    and
        touches the
    heart.
It speaks coldly
         and
     answers softly
     while whistling
   a tune of
the sun's rays.
Kissing the galaxy
   and warming the
     seas
       it opens
    all feeling
   and greed.
It tackles the
    mind
and touches
the bones.

—Amy DuRoss

Writing has grown naturally from the experience of exploring *Origins* in the classroom. The clusters of vocabulary that share images, the alliterative play of sound found in many of the word families, the inventiveness with sound and meaning revealed by many word histories, the use of images and experience to express ideas in lively ways that catch the mind's eye—these elements fundamental to how language grows are natural resources for writing. In addition, many word family chapters in this book present specific writing ideas. These are based both on the words of the family and on the poetry included in the chapter. Writing ideas that can be used with any of the families are found in the "Writing" section of the "Using *Origins*" chapter.

Exploring the *Origins* word families can also be a resource for "getting the picture" in reading. Understanding how we seize the images and details from our experience to express ideas illuminates the meaning not only in individual words, but in poems and stories and histories as well. Students who have explored how the root image "to shine" was used to express an idea of happiness in the word *glad* have a feel for how the more extended images of Paul Vesey's poem express a feeling of celebration:

American Gothic
to Satch

Sometimes I feel like I will *never* stop
Just go on forever
Til one fine mornin'
I'm gonna reach up and grab me a handfulla stars
Swing out my long lean leg
And whip three hot strikes burnin' down the heavens
And look over at God and say
How about that!

What feelings are evoked by the scene that opens Madeleine L'Engle's *A Wrinkle in Time*?

> In her attic bedroom Margaret Murry, wrapped in an old patchwork quilt, sat at the foot of her bed and watched the trees tossing in the frenzied lashing of the wind. Behind the trees clouds scudded frantically across the sky. Every few moments the moon ripped through them, creating wraith-like shadows that raced along the ground.

In the following lines from Gwyneth Morgan's *Life in a Medieval Village*, do Robert Fitzralph and the sheriff represent only themselves, or are they presented as a way of pointing beyond themselves to general realities of the medieval world?

> As part of his duty as a tenant, John has to help mend the road that runs through the village. Like most lords, Robert Fitzralph does not take much interest in the work and thinks it a great nuisance and expense and waste of time. But since the sheriff's horse stumbled in a rut a few years back, and the sheriff hurt his arm and lost his temper, the lord feels obliged to do something about repairing the worst parts of the road each autumn. All the tenants are pressed into service to quarry and cut the stones and to fill up the holes and ruts.

"Getting the picture" as we read often requires having a sense of how meaning moves beyond specific and literal details to suggest larger ideas. This movement takes place in many various ways. Sometimes it involves formal metaphor—as it often does in poetry—but sometimes it involves a looser, less formal process of pointing beyond specifics to more general ideas—as in the story of Robert Fitzralph and the sheriff.

As students learn how meaning moves from experience to idea in individual words, they begin to extend that understanding to poetry, stories, and nonfiction.

Using *Origins*:
The Teaching Materials in Volume 2

Overview

In Volume 2 of *Origins*, each chapter presents material for introducing and exploring a word family. Most chapters also provide poetry that includes images or concepts of the word family and writing ideas based either on the poetry or on playing with words and images of the family. All chapters include material for exploring how concrete meanings are extended to express abstract and figurative ideas, and many chapters include a specific section called "Exploring Extended Meanings" that details ways of making the process clear. Before reading further, you should browse through one or two word families, since we refer to them often in the following pages.

The teaching materials presented with each word family may have a somewhat formal look, but they are meant to be used as a flexible resource and adapted to your own needs and interests. We found that the clearest way of presenting the material was one that preserved a sense of conversation—of us talking with you and of you talking with your students. The format is *not* meant to be a script. It is meant, rather, to evoke a sense of the lively exchange between students and teachers that has in fact taken place as they explored the word families together. The format allows us to use a light touch in presenting a lot of specific information: information about the history of individual words in a family; thoughts on how to clarify the connection between a word's origin and its present meaning; ideas for ways of bringing the material to life through skits and pantomime, through exploring objects, and through helping students explore and remember experiences of their own that illuminate the meaning of a word.

In Volume 2, teaching ideas are presented in considerable detail in the beginning chapters and in more abbreviated form as the later chapters progress. In the "Developing Your Own Word Families" section at the end of this chapter, we discuss how you might explore word families not included in *Origins*.

Introducing *Origins*

How do you begin using *Origins*? Do you plunge straight in to exploring one of the word families? Most teachers like to provide a brief introduction to the overall idea of word families first.

Vergaline Campbell, a teacher in the District of Columbia public schools, introduced the idea of word families by comparing them to family reunions. What similarities can be seen among relatives at a family reunion? She gave an example from her own family: the "Campbell eyes" and "Campbell mouth" that led one relative to say, "I could tell a Campbell anywhere." Then she talked about how, in tracing the lines of relationship in a family, people sometimes construct a family tree. She drew an example of a family tree on the board, and that became the point of reference for introducing the word tree and the concepts it represents:

- Just as new people are born into a family, creating new and larger families, new words grow from older "parent" words.
- Just as new members of a family resemble parents and grandparents in certain ways, members of a word family resemble the older "parent" word or root in certain ways. Members of a word family resemble each other through a shared meaning of the "parent" root and through a shared spelling pattern.
- Just as members of a human family have many individual differences as well as many shared traits, members of a word family have distinct individual definitions, as well as a shared connection to the same root meaning and spelling pattern.

Many teachers have used some version of this family reunion idea as a way of introducing *Origins*.

Others have begun by exploring items of popular speech current in students' own language. They explored items such as *rip off* and *chill out*, looking at how the idea expressed by *rip off* (stealing, or cheating someone out of something) grew from the image of separation and the suggestion of violence in the act of ripping, and how *chill out* (take it easy, relax) has its roots in the fact that substances move more slowly when chilled or cooled—hence, slowing down to relax. Teachers exploring such items of popular speech might discuss them along the following lines:

You've just discovered a lot about the way language grows. Ever since language began, people have been making new words and expressions from old ones. They take some of the ideas from the old word and use them in new ways to create new words or phrases— the way someone created *rip off* from *rip*. Later, we're going to be looking at how many words grew in just that way.

Since popular speech changes rapidly, any examples we cite here will be quickly dated. If you want to introduce *Origins* via slang or expressions particular to a region or culture, you will need to be alert to what is current among your own students. Choose expressions whose origins are relatively obvious. (See the "Exploring Popular Speech" and "Cross-Cultural Metaphors" sections toward the end of this chapter for further discussion.) Using students' own speech to introduce *Origins* can be particularly powerful for students who have negative or ambivalent feelings about school. One teacher found that this approach was also very effective in her English as a Second Language class, because her students were delighted to learn some "American expressions."

Some teachers like to introduce *Origins* by drawing on the material presented in the "A Brief History of the English Language" chapter. Although the historical background is *not* necessary for exploring the word families, it is helpful for answering questions as they may arise. Beyond that, use the history in whatever ways may be appropriate or appealing for your own students—or skip it.

Introducing Word Families to Students

In each of the introductions to the individual word families in Volume 2, our focus is on showing how word meanings arise from the images of our experience. In presenting ideas for exploring how words developed from a particular root image or experience, we have tried to preserve the playfulness of the process. Have fun with the material. Entering into the playful spirit that underlies the birth of new words and meanings and developing a delight in language have down-to-earth results for students, not the least of which is a love of reading and writing. Keep this thought foremost in your mind as you introduce word families; it is more important than any particular idea presented

in the material. Better to skip something than to lose the spirit of adventure through worrying about every detail.

Here are principles to keep in mind as you use the material—and adapt it to your own purposes:

- Bring the imagery of the root to life at the outset by relating it to something concrete and familiar to your students.
- Keep things clear visually. As you go along, put the root and its meaning and the words of the family on the board in such a way that the relationships among them are obvious.
- Be sure students understand the connection between the root image or experience and the modern meaning of individual words in the family.
- Be sure students notice the other point of connection (a shared spelling pattern or sound pattern) that links the root and the words that have grown from it.
- Have students get word meanings "in their bones" through exploring objects, doing skits and pantomimes, and discussing examples of how the meanings are embodied in their own experience.

The particular ideas suggested for introducing the words of a family have evolved from the experience of using *Origins* in the classroom.   These ideas can be used directly or as a starting point for your own ideas. We couldn't resist including more insights and information about some words than you will want to use in any one session—especially when you are just getting acquainted with the material. These "extras" can be included at a later time, if you wish. As you prepare for introducing a particular word family, you may find it helpful to develop a summary image for each of the words in the family rather than trying to remember ideas for introducing them in linear form. For example, you can summarize our suggestion for a pantomime to introduce the word *bold* by visualizing students crouching and hiding from danger and then standing, taking a deep breath, looking as fearsome as possible, and boldly advancing to meet the danger (*bold* comes from a root that means "to swell"). It takes a lot of words to *describe* the images, but the images themselves summarize many words.

Doing pantomimes, examining objects, and discussing how word meanings are embodied in students' own experiences can all be used either to introduce words or to investigate a word's meaning and connection to the root after it has been introduced. We have found that students enjoy discovering the words of a family for themselves. Once they have the root and two or three words of the family, they enjoy using the clues of shared imagery and shared spelling pattern, as well as pantomime, etc., to discover other words of the family. Any words that do share the imagery and spelling pattern but turn out not to be actual members of the family can be included as "sound cousins" (discussed below). Some teachers prefer to introduce the whole family first and use the teaching suggestions to explore connections between the root and the word family later. Whichever approach you may use, you will find that, after students have explored several word families and have a feel for the process, they will begin leaping ahead of any step-by-step introduction of words to generate many words of the family—and a number of "sound cousins" as well—in one quick burst. Let the suggestions flow and investigate connections between word and root as the next step. If suggestions become too random, ask students to describe a connection with the imagery of the root as they propose each word. You do want to keep the focus on *how* new words and meanings develop.

The word family chapters are loosely ordered in terms of the complexity of the material presented. The beginning chapters present core linguistic ideas and later chapters build on this base. Teaching ideas, on the other hand, are spelled out in greatest detail in the first few chapters, then presented in briefer form as the chapters progress. We suggest you start with one of the early chapters, then follow whatever order best suits your class.

How long should you spend exploring any given word family? Most teachers have spent at least two class sessions of approximately forty-five minutes on a given word family—usually in once-a-week sessions. The amount of time you spend will depend, of course, on the age of your students and on what materials and activities you find appropriate for your class. Teachers who have used the writing ideas presented in the word family chapters and elsewhere in this chapter have generally done so during class periods normally allotted for writing—and the time spent on writing may be in addition to two sessions for exploring the family itself. Teachers working with older students have sometimes focused primarily on writing and have spent no more than half an hour on an introductory exploration of the family.

We have found that the greatest value of the material lies in fully under-standing the ideas in it, not in racing through as many word families as possible.

Therefore, whatever materials you choose to use, we urge you to keep in mind that their fundamental value lies not in providing a "vocabulary" list, but rather in awakening a feeling for words that will change how students read, write, talk, and think.

Sound Cousins

"Sound cousin" is a term we coined to describe a relationship based on sound patterns, not family descent. Many word families in *Origins* include groups of words that share the same beginning sounds. For example, most of the words of the GHEL family are alliterative: *gleam, glow, glimmer, glisten, glint, glass, glossy,* and *glad.* Because English has this large group of *gl-* words that share the imagery of shining (their root meaning), we have a tendency to associate other *gl-* words with images of light, as well—if their meanings allow such association. For instance, students frequently—and quite insistently—argue that *glory* and *glorious* should be members of the GHEL family. They point out that a glorious day is usually one full of sunshine, that those who achieve glory usually "shine" in what they do. (Unmentioned so far by students, but supporting the association, are the many links between light and glory in religious art and language.) Since *glory* and *glorious* do share with the GHEL words both a sound pattern and the imagery of shining, it is legitimate to affirm the connection that students intuitively feel as they argue for including the words in the family. We have coined the term "sound cousins" to describe the connection. Linguists use other terms (such as "sound symbolism") to describe the connection, but do recognize it as real. However, the tendency to associate the imagery of the GHEL family with other *gl-* words is just that— a tendency. *Gloomy* and *glum* both begin with *gl-* , but their ending sounds and their meanings cut the association short.

In the word family chapters in Volume 2, we include notes on sound cousins that have frequently been proposed by students. The word trees in those chapters include both space for recording the words of the family and a space at the side of the tree for sound cousins. When deciding whether words may be recognized as sound cousins, you need to consider whether they share both a sound pattern and an area of imagery or meaning.

Additional Related Words

At the beginning of each chapter, we list the words we most commonly introduce as members of a particular word family. There are often more words in the family than in that list. We omit words from the introductory list for a variety of reasons, usually because they are of less immediate interest than the core words of the group. Many words left out of the introductory list are listed at the end of each chapter under "Additional Related Words." Depending on the age and interests of your students, you may want to include some or all of the "Additional Related Words" as you explore the family.

For a definitive list of all members of a word family, check the "Indo-European Root Appendix" of the 1969 edition of *The American Heritage Dictionary of the English Language,* which may well be in your library, or the updated version of the "Appendix" published in 1985 under the title of *The American Heritage Dictionary of Indo-European Roots*, as a companion to the 1982 *Second College Edition of the American Heritage Dictionary.* If you look up word families in these sources, you will find that we have omitted certain words because of their general obscurity, a sound shift that requires a lot of arcane explanation, or an overcomplicated history of development. Because some roots have been adapted for *Origins*, you should read the "Word of Explanation" note in the "Linguistic Background" chapter before doing such research.

Wrap-up and Review

Discussed below are materials and activities you can use after you have introduced the words of a family. Teachers have often found it useful to have students assemble their own *Origins* notebooks where they keep word trees, illustrations, definitions, and story puzzles, as well as poetry and their own writing.

Word Trees

Word trees can provide a clear visual summary of the relationship between the root and the words that grew from it. Each word has a relationship to the root, but has branched off to establish its own distinct meaning. At the end of each volume of *Origins*, you will find a word tree that can be photocopied for students. The tree includes space at the bottom for recording the root and

Individual word tree (*right*)
and class word tree (*below*)

24

its meaning, spaces in the branches for recording words of the family, and space at the side of the tree for recording sound cousins.

Many teachers also have used a large word tree posted on a bulletin board. Students record the words on index cards and hang them on the tree. Some classrooms have made smaller poster-paper word trees for each family, gradually accumulating a "forest" of trees over the course of the year. The "forest" keeps the words of the family readily available as a resource for writing.

Illustrations

Asking students to use the words of a family by drawing a "picture that tells a story" can help integrate the words with their own experience and imagination. The teachers in our workshops who have expressed doubt about the value of the exercise, usually say, after doing the exercise, "Aha, you really *do* learn a lot...."

You might start by brainstorming ideas for illustrations with the class. The brainstorming alone can be a good exercise. In doing the illustrations, the emphasis should be on ideas, not perfect artwork. Speech "balloons" (like those in comic books and comic strips) can enlarge the possibilities for expressing ideas. You may want to give students the choice of working in small groups to do group illustrations together. You might want to join a group and get a feel for the process yourself. Students often enjoy showing their illustrations to each other.

Story Puzzles

Many word families include story puzzles that can provide another opportunity for playing with the words of the family. These can be done in groups or individually, as part of classwork or for extra credit. An alternative to doing the puzzles in a straightforward manner is to put the *wrong* words in the blanks, an experiment that can illuminate the words in surprising ways because of their shared imagery.

Definitions

We have provided our own brief definitions of words in each family. These definitions focus on meanings explored in the *Origins* materials, often highlighting connections with the root imagery of the family. Although you can have students look up their own definitions, you can save time by putting ours on the board for students to copy.

Student illustrations based on the WER and GHEIS roots.

Review Pantomimes

Most teachers spend at least two sessions on a given word family. Many have found that at the start of a second session students enjoy reintroducing and reviewing the words of a family by inventing their own pantomimes. Such pantomimes often inspire imaginative thinking about the words. Sometimes when the teacher has difficulty figuring out what word is being dramatized, the students are quick to identify it.

Exploring Extended Meanings

The "Exploring Extended Meanings" sections discuss how primary meanings, grounded in experience, are extended to express abstract and figurative ideas. We use the term *extended meaning* and, in student materials, the phrase *stretch the meaning*, to focus attention on this process instead of focusing on the labels used to identify the results of the process—metaphor, abstraction, figurative language, etc. You may use any labels familiar to your students, but keep in mind that the primary value of "Exploring Extended Meanings" lies in having students get the feel of the process by walking through it and focusing on how it happens rather than on how to label it.

Students are, of course, already familiar with how the imagery of root meanings has been extended to create new words and meanings. In families made up largely of Germanic vocabulary, most words have primary meanings that remain grounded in everyday experience. "Exploring Extended Meanings" follows the evolution of these words into the realm of ideas. In general, it is only in the Germanic vocabulary of the language that we see both concrete and abstract levels of meaning in the same word—both the down-to-earth *clamp* holding two boards together and the police *clamping down* on speeders, both the *glimmer* of a candle in a dark room and the *glimmer* of an idea in our minds. By contrast, much of our Latin-based vocabulary is already "extended" or abstract. (See the "Brief History of the English Language" chapter for further discussion.)

"Exploring Extended Meanings," then, takes a look at "home-grown" abstractions that occur in the development of words in the KER, GHEL, FLEU, KEL, and WER families. The exploration of abstraction in these families provides a model for exploring "extended meanings" wherever you may encounter them—elsewhere in *Origins* and in whatever reading your students may be doing in class.

Reading Poetry

Most of the word family chapters include poetry that uses the imagery of the family. Poetry flows naturally from the imagery and metaphor inherent in how new words and meanings take shape. The poems that accompany word families include both student poetry written in response to writing ideas that accompany a family and adult poetry. The adult poetry ranges from ancient to modern and includes traditional African and Native American poetry, African-American poetry and poetry from Japan, poetry translated from Russian and from Chinese, poetry from seventeenth-century England and from twentieth-century America. Three poems were written especially for *Origins* by Kate Rushin, a Boston poet. A few families are not accompanied by poetry because we could not find any that used the images or words of the family in ways we found inviting or compelling. You should, of course, feel free to add other poems.

As with all of *Origins*, these examples are meant to be used flexibly. You may use one or two poems with one word family and none with another; you may settle in with a feast of several poems if you find a group that is particularly irresistible. The poems can be used in many ways. They can be read aloud: by you, by individual students, or by students in choral groups. Some, such as "Legend" (in the BHEL family), can be acted out. Others, such as "The Rapper as Light" (in the GHEL family), invite memorization and chanting. Some lend themselves to illustration. The poetry can also be used to inspire students to do their own writing.

Writing and Ideas for Other Activities

We have found that the vocabulary of *Origins* begins to animate students' writing, whether or not we make formal attempts to make it do so. You may want to leave it at that. For those who would like to go beyond casual connections with writing, we present writing ideas particular to the words and poetry of specific families and other ideas that can be used generally with any family.

The writing ideas in the word family chapters create a sense of listening in on a classroom conversation, which you should adapt for your own purposes.

A good general approach to writing is that described by Flora Arnstein in her books *Poetry and the Child* (New York: Dover, 1962) and *Children Write Poetry* (New York: Dover, 1967). Her gentle approach focuses first on awakening children's understanding of the elements of poetry by inviting them to make choices. In discussing poems, she asks, "What are your favorite lines, words, sounds, pictures?" When prompted to make their own judgments, children begin to look closely and listen carefully. Arnstein also invites students to choose which poems they want to keep for their own personal anthology. Students feel empowered and independent when rejecting poems that don't move them and accepting ones that do. After exploring their favorite elements of two or three poems and choosing what they want to include in their own anthology, the students write. No particular instructions are necessary. Students simply are given free time to write their own poem or story. What Arnstein finds (as we have found in using the approach) is that students reach for what they can use in the poetry they've read and use it as best suits their needs. It may be an emotion or idea they want to explore, or words or sounds they want to play with. Alternatively, the inspiration may be subterranean and indirect—something is nudged awake by a chain of associations and comes to the surface, seeking a shape. Arnstein usually publishes the students' writing so they can read each other's work.

If you want to follow this approach with *Origins*, you will give students all or most of the poems that accompany a given family so that students can choose among them for their own anthology. In addition to having students choose their favorite poems, you may want to have them choose their favorite words of a family.

Many other writing teachers have used model poems to inspire their students to write. Among the best examples are Kenneth Koch's *Rose, Where Did You Get That Red?* (New York: Vintage, 1974) and Nina Nyhart and Kinereth Gensler's *The Poetry Connection* (New York: Teachers & Writers Collaborative, 1978).

Some teachers have used *Origins* primarily as a resource for writing. Larry Fagin, a writer-in-the-schools, has focused on the imagery of the families to generate vocabularies that serve as inspiration for students' poetry. When using the GHEL ("to shine") family, for example, he first invites students to generate and explore the words of the family and then to brainstorm other words that share in the imagery of "shining." All possibilities are welcomed: *sparkle, sun, diamond, firecracker, shimmer, bright, fire, flame, lightning, polish, ruby, torch, mica, sunset.* The next step is to brainstorm opposites—"dark" words: *shadow, cave, cloudy, dull, midnight, sad, dreary, twilight, black hole, shady, purple, fading*—whatever comes to mind. After a large vocabulary of "shining" and "dark" words has been generated on the board, Fagin reads a few poems by students who have done a similar exercise, writes a collaborative poem with the class, and then launches the students on their own poems and stories.

Here are some additional ideas and other activities proposed by writers at Teachers & Writers Collaborative.

- Have students combine words from a single family (such as *gladglass* from the GHEL family or *drizzledroopy* from DERU) and use them in their writing. Such amalgamations, especially from Germanic roots, suggest vivid images that might serve as the radiant center of new student poems.

- Have each student pick a word (*glimmer, belly, drizzle*), pantomime it, and then anthropomorphize it by giving it a name (Cherie Glimmer, Marvin Belly, Manuel Drizzle) and creating a character for it. Then perhaps have the kids write monologues, dialogues, or short plays using these characters. Such dramatic pieces are usually more sucessful if they involve a conflict.

- Choose a word and have students design a kind of "happening" for it, for example, a Glimmer Event in which all the students hold mirrors and bright flashlights in a dark room.

- Have students form living word trees, like an acrobatic or cheerleading team. One student plays the root, the others are arranged above him or her in the branches. (The best way might be to have the "branches" standing and sitting on a table and the "root" hunkered down on the floor.) Then they all simultaneously act out their words, using sound and movement.

• As a corollary to the above, have the same students create spontaneous sentences that link together, as in the example given below. This is just a variation on the old idea of spontaneous oral stories, with the added rule of using words from a single family.

> Example (using KER words):
> Student 1: "The burglar *crept* around the..."
> Student 2: "...uh, the *crooked* tree where..."
> Student 3: "...some *creepy* people were..."
> Student 4: "...*crocheting* a..."
> Student 5: "...picture of a *creek*..."
> Student 6: "...on a *cradle* pillow."

• Have students invent a word or words for experiences or feelings they've had, but for which there is no obvious, specific word. Say you are ten years old and you've wanted a particular toy for years. Now your parents have finally promised it to you for your birthday, but when that day comes, they give you something you don't even want! You feel both deflated and explosive. Invent a word that stands for that feeling. Then write an account of the incident, using the invented word or words. Of course, the event could also be a happy one—for example, a moment when someone you liked or admired suddenly and unexpectedly showed warmth toward you.

• Have students write a dialogue in an imaginary language. For instance, two young people, Arprizal and Colinet, meet at midnight in the town of Rogovekail. Both of them are very sad:

> ARPRIZAL: Soling to vog butig nott.
> COLINET: Fentig soling butig regonott.
> ARPRIZAL: Fo, fo nott moto pur copi.
> COLINET: Vog butig solig soling.
> ARPRIZAL: Vog butig nog.
> COLINET: Fentig nog soling.

They leave together, arm in arm, happier but still a little anxious.

- Have some students make a dictionary of the words in the dialogue above. Have other students translate the dialogue into English, with or without the dictionary.

- Have students invent the future form of contemporary words, and write sentences, poems, stories, etc., using these words. The notion of the possible future of words makes more sense if the students have an idea of how certain contemporary words are themselves products of verbal evolution. So, for example, if *God be with you* was gradually condensed to *goodbye*, perhaps the next step will involve even further condensation, to something like *gdbi*. If *goodnesse* became *goodness*, then perhaps it will be slimmed down to *goodnes*. If *breakfast* + *lunch* created *brunch*, will *lunch* + *dinner* create *linner*? (Probably not, because *linner* doesn't sound appealing.) And how about new words to describe new things? Will there be "feelovision"? A "telerose"? A "megadog"? Will the troublesome apostrophe (*it's* versus *its*) disappear? Creating a plausible-sounding future English involves a certain amount of thinking and analysis, not just a spewing forth of gibberish (which is fun, too).

Developing Your Own Word Families

How did we develop ideas for exploring word families in the classroom? And how can you develop similar approaches to word families not in this book? First, you need to think of the root meaning of a family not as a word or words on the page, but as an experience. What experience does the "meaning" of the root evoke? How can the meaning be embodied? Once you develop a full sense of the root experience, the ways in which words of the family embody facets of the experience begin to come to life for you. Then you can begin to think of ways to highlight those connections and dramatize how the experience takes shape in particular words. Dramatizing an individual word may be no more "dramatic" than discussing with students examples of its meaning in their own lives. What you're trying to get is that grounding in experience that yields a full-bodied sense of a word's meaning.

If you are exploring words of Germanic origin, you will often be tracing three stages of development: the root meaning; a primary, concrete meaning; and an extended, figurative meaning. The primary meaning will be the resource for seeing how the figurative meaning—or meanings—developed. If you are exploring words of Latin or Greek origin, you may find it helpful to remember that, although most of these words have an abstract meaning in English, many of them also had a concrete meaning in their native setting. Sometimes imagining what that meaning might have been conjures up a scene from the past. For example, a *report* is, literally, something "carried back." Pondering that meaning, the mind can travel back to a time before telephones or airplanes and visualize a messenger arriving on foot with a piece of news. Thinking about the imagery of something "carried back," one can also understand the connection between a rifle report and a report on the state of the economy.

Dictionaries

When preparing to explore a word family, we use dictionaries a lot. Our starting point is the "Appendix" of the 1969 *American Heritage Dictionary* or the 1985 *American Heritage Dictionary of Indo-European Roots*, cited above. We have listed additional families drawn from this resource in the "Linguistic Background" chapter. If you want to focus on developing word families of

Latin and Greek origin, two excellent pamphlets are Rudolf Schaeffer's *Latin-English Derivative Dictionary* and *The Greek-English Derivative Dictionary*, both available from the American Classical League (Miami University, Oxford, Ohio 45056). We also refer to *The Oxford English Dictionary* to check on how words of a family have developed over time. The *OED* provides dated quotations that exemplify how words were used, some dating back to the ninth century. We skim the quotations and the archaic and obsolete meanings of a word to see how its imagery has been used to express a variety of meanings. A revised, updated version of *The Oxford English Dictionary* was published in twenty volumes in 1989. We use the *Compact Edition of the Oxford English Dictionary* (New York: Oxford University Press, 1971) because of its convenience and relatively low cost. The *Compact Edition* micrographically reduces the thirteen volumes of the original dictionary (published in 1933) to two volumes that must be read with a magnifying glass (which comes with the volumes). Supplements updating the dictionary are produced in a third compact volume.

In addition to *The American Heritage Dictionary* and the *OED*, *The Random House Dictionary of the English Language* (New York: Random House, 1969 and 1987) and *The Oxford Dictionary of English Etymology* (Oxford, New York, 1966) are very useful. We also consult student dictionaries for clarity and simplicity in word definitions. The two we have used most frequently are the *Scott Foresman Intermediate Dictionary* (Glenview, Illinois: Scott, Foresman, 1988) and the *Houghton Mifflin Intermediate Dictionary* (Boston: Houghton Mifflin, 1986). Both dictionaries are good for students, as well, because they contain many word histories. All these resources are fun to share with older students—fifth and sixth graders, even fourth graders. Simply put the dictionaries out for whoever may be interested. Some students are fascinated and enjoy leafing through the pages. Pursuing words in the *OED* with a magnifying glass is a special favorite. Other students don't want to venture near such weighty tomes and shouldn't be required to. The point is to convey a sense of adventure, not pedantry.

How Meanings Change over Time

As you explore word histories, you will often find that the connections between root meanings and current meanings are illuminating and readily understandable. At times, however, the path of development may seem puzzling—or even illogical. The word *nice*, for example, once meant "ignorant, foolish" and the word *silly* once meant "happy, blessed." People sometimes cite such word histories as examples of how word meaning develops by unpredictable—and, by implication, mysterious—leaps. Although the ways in which meanings develop from a particular root or image cannot be predicted, they are almost always understandable in retrospect if you know something about the history and circumstances in which the new meaning took shape.

If you are puzzled by a particular shift of meaning, *The Oxford English Dictionary*, with its abundance of historical information, can often help. For example, the *OED* provides clues to why *nice* evolved from meaning "ignorant, foolish" in the 1200s to meaning "pleasant, agreeable" today. Citations from the 1500s and 1600s use *nice* to mean "tender, delicate." A leap of imagination allows us to see that the qualities of being ignorant and foolish might be seen in affectionate or indulgent terms when looking at a young child, for example, and therefore associated with a kindly attitude toward vulnerability. Once we feel kindly and indulgent toward vulnerable creatures, we can readily shift from focusing on their foolishness to focusing on their tenderness and delicacy. That is one shift toward a positive meaning of *nice*. For citations of *nice* from the 1600s and 1700s, the *OED* gives the meaning of "over-refined, luxurious." One can readily see an association between foolishness or ignorance and pretentious attempts at refinement and luxury (the concept of *nouveau riche* is an old one). Gradually, however, positive qualities associated with refinement and luxury predominated, and the association with foolishness and ignorance dropped away. Over the centuries, then, the word *nice* became associated with a variety of positive qualities. Its evolution from meaning "foolish and ignorant" to meaning "pleasant and agreeable" becomes understandable once you know the intermediate steps of development that took place between the eleventh and the twentieth centuries.

You can sometimes understand such shifts in meaning simply by using your imagination and understanding of human nature. When you stop to think about why *silly* might have evolved from its original meaning of "happy" or "blessed," you may be able to conjure up memories of people who have seemed foolishly and unrealistically happy or "blissed out." A term from the 1960s, "bliss ninnies," embodies precisely the combination of ecstasy and accompanying divorce from reality (and hence foolishness with regard to practical reality) that seems the likely pivot on which the meaning of silly shifted from "happy" and "blessed" to "foolish."

Vegetate is another word that has, over time, embodied seemingly contradictory realities. In the 1600s the word was used to mean "to animate or quicken," "to make strong or vigorous"—meanings derived from the lively growth of plants and vegetables. By the mid-1700s, however, a different meaning grew from a different perspective on the vegetable world. *Vegetate* came to mean "to live a merely physical life; to lead a dull, monotonous existence." It is probably more than mere coincidence that this pejorative meaning of the word developed as the Industrial Revolution was beginning. Agrarian life no longer seemed so exciting to a world diverted by new industrial developments.

Linguists recognize many predictable routes by which meanings change, among them widening, narrowing, semantic shift, and semantic drift. An example of widening is the word *citizen*, which used to mean a city dweller and now means the inhabitant of a state or nation, and an example of narrowing is the word *meat*, which originally meant any solid food and now means a particular type. An example of semantic shift is the word *bureau*, which originally referred to a coarse woolen cloth over a desk, then to the desk itself (and by association other chests with drawers) and then to the organization that uses desks—as in the National Bureau of Standards. *Silly, foolish,* and *vegetate* are all examples of semantic drift. In *Origins* we focus on the stories that underlie such changes: the shift in power from the city-states of Greece to the empire of Rome that underlies the widening of the meaning of *citizen*, the growing diversity of foods available for eating that underlies the narrowing of the meaning of *meat*. We do not emphasize the linguistic terminology for these changes.

Exploring Popular Speech and
Cross-Cultural Metaphors

Popular speech and cross-cultural metaphors provide opportunities for affirming a student's own language, whatever that may be. All word meanings grow out of experience in ways similar to those presented in the word family chapters of Volume 2. Students can discover how their home or street language also grows out of experience. Consider having students make a list of expressions from their own slang or street talk and then speculate about their sources. (We conducted a similar session with a group of teachers in a summer workshop, the results of which are presented at the end of the "Linguistic Background" chapter. You can get a sense of the possibilities by looking at this material.)

As you and your students speculate on the origins of a particular expression, keep in mind that such origins are sometimes elusive. For instance, Frederic Cassidy and his colleagues, who are compiling the *Dictionary of American Regional English*, were trying to trace the expression "There's a dead cat on the line." They found that twenty people had cited the expression as meaning "Someone is trying to deceive you" or "Something fishy is going on," but no one knew its source. Only after many months did they find an old man in Louisiana who was able to explain that it came from an experience connected with catfishing in the bayou. Fishermen would leave trot lines in the bayou and come to check them every day. If someone checked a neighbor's line and found a dead catfish, he knew something was wrong, something was "fishy"— and he'd better check on his neighbor. "Something fishy is going on here" was generalized to a sense of "Someone is trying to deceive you"—a sense that wasn't present in the original experience. The researchers still aren't sure if this is the true history of "There's a dead cat on the line"; they were never able to confirm it through other sources. You can tell this story to your students as an example of how the source of an expression may be elusive.

More often, however, probable sources will suggest themselves fairly readily, as in the following: *crib* meaning "your house"; *chill* meaning "to cold shoulder"; *lunchin'* meaning "out of it"; *biting* meaning "copying"; and *jonesing* meaning "wanting something really badly." *Lunchin'* and *jonesing* seem to be interesting plays on the older expressions "out to lunch" and "keeping up with the Joneses" (acquiring what the neighbors have). *Biting* adds an aggressive thrust to the act of copying, opening up possibilities for boastful swagger in talking about something usually thought of in more furtive terms. *Chill* takes the image of coldness in a different direction from that of *chill out* (discussed above) and fits with numerous other images of coldness and warmth used to describe emotional states, as in: a warm friendship, a hot romance, a relationship that blows hot and cold, a lukewarm greeting, a cold look, a cool reception, an icy stare. These expressions reflect an intuitive understanding of the physics of excitement: molecules that are stirred to motion produce heat; as they subside toward stillness, things cool off. (Excitement can be positive, as in a *hot prospect*, or negative, as in *hot and bothered* or *boiling mad*. Likewise, lack of excitement can be positive, as in *keeping your cool* during an emergency, or negative, as in treating someone *coldly*.)

If you have students who speak languages other than English, you can explore whether there are similar metaphors based on heat and cold in their languages. Such metaphors seem to be widespread: we have found them in Spanish, Tagalog, Thai, and Hungarian. You can also explore metaphors based on the body. No matter how climate, geography, and custom may vary from one culture to another, we all experience the world through our bodies. That fundamental experience is reflected in all languages. Sometimes the metaphors are similar to ones we have in English, sometimes they are quite different. In Thai the metaphor that expresses what we mean when we say heartbroken is "chestbroken." In Tagalog a generous person is described as having an "open palm"—an image similar to the English *open-handed*. In Hungarian a clever person is an "eye-eared" person—not an expression with a close parallel in English but an image we can readily picture. In Temne a restless person, one who cannot settle down, is described by an expression that means "the foot keeps going."

A good way to begin exploring body metaphors in other languages is to brainstorm a list of such metaphors in English. You can use the "Body Metaphors in English" list at the end of the "Linguistic Background" chapter to generate ideas. Once you have made a list of English expressions, you can bring in expressions from other languages (those cited above, those in the "Bringing Words to Life" chapter, and any others from your own experience).

The combination will give students an idea of what to search for in their own language. Have them talk with their parents about the list of body metaphors, then tell the rest of the class what new ones they came up with.

You might want to see if metaphors in some of the word families are found in other languages, as well. For example, do other languages express the idea of happiness through images of light, as in *glad* (from GHEL, "to shine")? Are images of "up" and "down" used in other languages to express emotional states—as in the image of "falling" that underlies *dreary* in the DHREU family?

Sound and Meaning

"Sound cousins" alert students to a particular connection between sound and meaning—a connection between certain alliterative clusters and the imagery that becomes associated with them. You can play further with this association between sound and meaning by exploring the "sound families" listed in the "Linguistic Background" chapter. Most of these sound families have a core of words that come from a particular Indo-European root, but the most significant link among them is an initial consonant cluster that has an imitative quality. Such play with links between sound and meaning can, of course, be extended to other imitative words—*crunch, hiss, crackle, buzz, meow, thump, screech, whiz, rustle,* etc.

The following exercise can provide further insight into how the sounds of words influence our sense of their meaning. Use the pairs of "nonsense" words listed below and pose the following questions: Which is larger/smaller? Which is heavier/lighter? Which is quicker/slower?*

dobe	dabe
meeg	mog
scozzle	scuzzle
spant	spint
gleep	gloop

Provide students with a list of the nonsense words and read each pair aloud. Students usually have little hesitation about choosing a *dobe*, a *mog*, a *scozzle*, a *spant*, and a *gloop* as the larger, heavier, and slower members of their pairs. When asked to choose whether a *dobe* or a *dabe* is bigger, they usually have an immediate response and *know* which creature is bigger. (You might have your students imagine these nonsense names as creatures and then draw them.) It should be emphasized, however, that there are no right or wrong answers in this exercise.

The tendency to associate sound and meaning can readily be undercut and overridden by other associations. Although students usually associate the

---

*The concept of this exercise and some of the examples are drawn from *Origins of the English Language: A Social and Linguistic History* by Joseph M. Williams (New York: Macmillan, 1975).

"larger" sound with the larger creature, some students will find that the name *spant*, for example, evokes personal associations (the name of a pet mouse, a creature they saw in a cartoon) that lead them to decide that a *spant* is smaller than a *spint*—though the tendency of most students is to make the opposite choice. Links between sound and meaning operate in just this way. The sounds of a word nudge our sense of its meaning in certain directions—toward a sense of openness or a sense of constriction, toward a sense of sharpness or a sense of softness, toward a sense of liquid movement or a sense of movement blocked and cut short. (Students can have fun investigating such connections by making up their own pairs of nonsense names. Which is softer, a *mig* or a *mish*? Which moves more smoothly, a *smallow* or a *smatt*?) Such links between sound and meaning are real, but not definitive. Other associations can override them and move the meaning in another direction. Language can be particularly powerful, however, when both sound and meaning move in the same direction—as good poets have always known.

Sound and Spelling

In *Origins* we do not treat spelling systematically, but we do discuss certain spelling patterns, in the word family chapters of Volume 2, in the "Linguistic Background" chapter, and in the "Mixed Heritage of English" section of the "Brief History of English" chapter. One teacher commented that after her students had been immersed in *Origins* for a year, they shifted from considering English spelling an unreasonable burden to seeing it as an interesting story, though still a challenge. The value of the *Origins* materials that bear on spelling—information about vowel-*r* inversions and consonant shifts, about silent letters and varying patterns of pronunciation, about spelling patterns inherited from Anglo-Saxon, French, Latin, and Greek origins—lies in awakening such interest. Although none of the information provides a magic formula for remembering the spelling of particular words, making spelling an interesting story, not merely a rote task, can have practical results as well as intrinsic appeal.

A Brief History of the English Language

Why is the *k* of *know* not pronounced? Why is it there at all? What is the story behind the *-ture* of *nature*, the *-tion* of *station*, and the *ph-* of *photograph*? Behind the irregularities of English spelling lies a story of invasions—both military and cultural. As a result of those invasions, English vocabulary is a composite: Anglo-Saxon, or Old English*, the Germanic base; French, the language of the conquering Normans; and Latin, the language of scholars during the Renaissance. Words of Greek origin entered the language through Latin and later borrowings. The English we speak today echoes with the voices of diverse peoples and cultures. It has remained open to adopting new words whenever it rubs elbows with another language or dialect. American English has constantly enriched itself by drawing on the vocabularies and idioms of its many national and cultural groups.

In this chapter we look at the historical events that underlie the mixed heritage of English: the Anglo-Saxon invasions and settlement of Britain, the Viking incursions, the Norman Conquest, and the Renaissance. We then explain how the common ancestry of Anglo-Saxon (Old English), French, and Latin was discovered—and how that discovery provides resources for vocabulary study. Finally, we look at how various groups of Americans have contributed, and continue to contribute, to the growth of American English. It should be emphasized that we focus on only one part of the story of how English has developed—vocabulary. We do not describe the development of grammar. It should be emphasized, as well, that we sketch the history in broad outlines rather than in fine detail. Those who want to study the story of English in greater detail should see the annotated bibliography at the end of this chapter.

---

* Although "Old English" is the linguistically preferred term for English from A.D. 400 to the time of the Norman Conquest, we also use the term "Anglo-Saxon." "Old English" is confusing to students. As far as they're concerned, "Old English" might be the language their grandparents spoke. For students, the term "Anglo-Saxon" ties the language more clearly to the historical period in which it was current.

44

The Anglo-Saxon Invasions:
The Beginnings of English

Many of the common, everyday words in our language are Germanic in origin because, over a two-hundred-year period, England was invaded and settled by tribes from the area known today as Germany and Denmark. In the mid-400s Germanic tribes known as the Angles and the Saxons began leaving their homeland in northern Europe to seize the fertile and poorly defended coastal lands of southeast England. England had been part of the Roman Empire—a land inhabited by Celts, but ruled by the Romans who had conquered them. In the early fifth century, however, the Roman troops were called back to defend the heart of the Empire against the wave of barbarian invasions flooding across Europe. The Celts were left without a strong defense.

Anglo-Saxon Invasion and Settlement of England
ca. 450-600

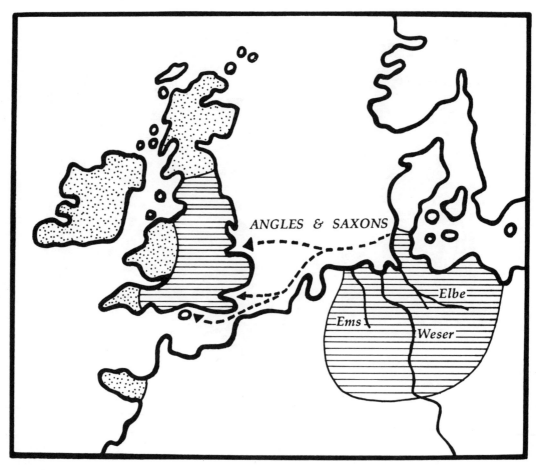

 CELTS

 ANGLES & SAXONS

Other Germanic tribes—probably Jutes, Frisians, and Franks—accompanied the Angles and the Saxons in relatively small numbers, but the invaders came to be generally known as Saxons, or Anglo-Saxons, because these were the dominant tribes. The invaders got a toehold in the southeast corner of Britain and then began pushing outward in all directions, settling and tilling the land as they won it. The spreading conquest was brought to a temporary halt by one last great Celtic victory. Unified and rallied by a leader, who was probably the legendary King Arthur, the Celts defeated the Saxons at Mount Badon, a strategic height somewhere in south-central Britain.

The victory gave the Celts two generations of peace. Then the Anglo-Saxons began advancing once again. Most Celts began their final retreat into the far corners of the island—areas today known as Scotland, Wales, and Cornwall. Some migrated even further. One tribe, the Britons, from whom we get the name Britain, resettled in the northwest corner of France now known as Brittany. Breton minstrels preserved the old Celtic tale of King Arthur and later, as minstrels in the courts of the Norman conquerors, brought the tale back to England.

By the end of the sixth century, then, most of England (from Angleland, or land of the Angles) was in Anglo-Saxon hands. The Celts who remained in the conquered territory began to speak the languages of their Saxon overlords. Like the language of the Indians in America, the language of the Celts in England left its trace primarily in the form of place names such as Avon, the Welsh word for "river."

Although the Germanic tribes who settled England spoke a variety of dialects, they could understand one another. The Germanic language of the island came to be known as Anglo-Saxon, later as Angle-ish or Engle-ish (language of the Angles) and, finally, as English. From this "language of the Angles" come our words for the basics of life: *eat, sleep, bread, drink, meat, love, hate, sun, father, rain, earth, mother, birth, death, speak, walk, sing, child, friend, flesh, bone, foot, hand, head, heart, soul, seed, crop, tree, stone, sea, fish, bird, fire, ash, ask, give, bless, curse, heal, rise, fall, float, deep, high, strong, weak, weave, knit, churn, plow, bake, brew, bubble, breathe.*

Old Norse: Some Closely Related Germanic Words Are Added to Anglo-Saxon Vocabulary

A new invasion brought a new influx of words. During the latter part of the Viking Age (850-1050), Anglo-Saxon was enriched by words from Old Norse, the Germanic language of the Danish Vikings who invaded and settled parts of England. Where speakers of Anglo-Saxon and Old Norse lived side by side, many became bilingual, especially those who intermarried. When both languages were spoken in the same communities and the same houses, they influenced each other. Many Old Norse words flowed into Anglo-Saxon, or Old English. Because Old Norse and Old English both came from the same Germanic ancestor, words from both sources are often very much of the same mold.

Like the words of Old English, the Danish words inherited by English tend to be associated with everyday life: *bark, blunder, cozy, dawn, egg, flake, gale, gift, happy, knife, kindle, law, loan, loose, loom, mistake, muggy, outlaw, rake, raise, rot, spray, stack, swirl, tangle, thrift, tight, want, wing, window*. Many *sk-* and *sc-* words in the language come from Old Norse: *scalp, scare, scold, scorch, scout, scowl, scrape, scream, scuffle, skate, ski, skid, skill, skin, skip, skirt, skit, sky*.

The Norman Conquest:
French Becomes the Language of
the Ruling Class in England

In the eleventh century the Anglo-Saxons were driven from all important positions of power by French-speaking conquerors, the Normans. The Normans (the name derives from *Norsemen*) were of Viking ancestry, but had adopted French language and culture after forming an alliance with the French king and settling in northern France in what we now call Normandy. The Norman conquest of England was an unlikely one that succeeded through many turns of luck.

In 1066 William, Duke of Normandy, who came to be known as William the Conqueror, gathered troops and ships in the estuary of the River Dives in northwest France. He was related to the English royal family and had laid claim to the English throne. The English had ignored his claim, and now he set forth to seize the throne by force.

The Norman Invasion of England, 1066

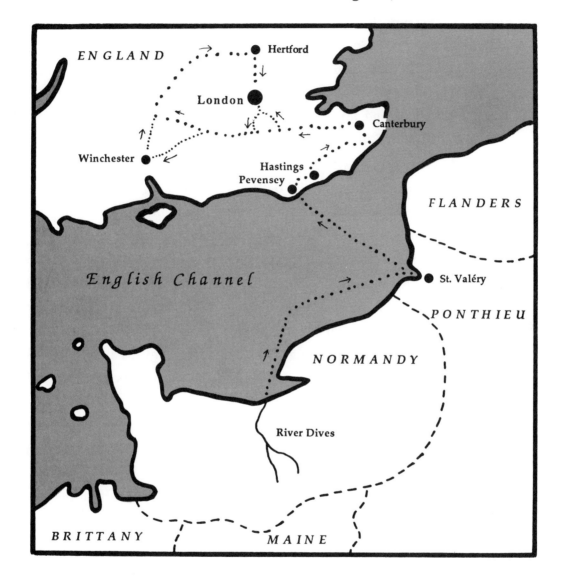

Few Normans expected William to succeed. His plan of invasion was considered foolhardy. It depended on luck—a wind to blow his ships straight for a good English harbor. Weather prediction, hardly reliable now, was wholly unreliable then. The Norman fleet was neither equipped to row nor to tack; the ships could only sail before the wind, and any shift of wind could scatter the invaders. Because the Normans had forgotten the seafaring arts of their Viking ancestors and had settled into a feudal life on land, they were not skilled sailors. In addition, the feudal nobles had adopted the French style of fighting on horseback. William's plan of invasion, then, called for unskilled sailors to transport both troops and horses in unwieldy boats.

The risky nature of his plan shaped the army he gathered. The Norman barons owed William approximately forty days of military service a year, but they were quick to decide that feudal duty did not include a reckless overseas adventure. William raised only part of his army from among his barons. The rest were paid soldiers lured by the hope of pillaging England.

As it happened, luck rode with the Normans, though few would have recognized their first run of luck as good. On September 12, the Norman ships ran the ebb tide out of the Dives estuary and sailed before a south wind toward England. Then disaster struck, or so it seemed. The wind shifted, a gale rose, the fleet scattered. Storm winds blew ships eastward along the rocky Norman coast, where some foundered on the rocks. Survivors edged into the first safe harbor they came to, St. Valéry.

Refusing to heed common wisdom—autumn storms had begun, the sailing season was at an end—William held his army on the beaches of St. Valéry for two weeks, waiting for the next favorable wind.

During those weeks, the English army, which had been guarding the coast against probable invasion, went home. The English had known of William's plan for some time, but considered the autumn storms a sure defense against further threat that year.

As the army dispersed, King Harold of England was called north to quell a Viking invasion led by King Harald of Norway. Raising his army as he went, the English king marched north in record time, took the Viking king by surprise, and defeated the invaders decisively. Legend has it that the English were celebrating at a victory feast when word came that William had landed on the English coast. Against all odds, when the equinox had passed and winter gales were to be expected, William had gotten a favorable wind that held steady for the whole of his crossing. Nine hundred years have passed since the Norman invasion, and no invader has copied its success.

King Harold came south by a forced march. At the Battle of Hastings, he was killed (by an arrow through the eye, we are told) and the English were defeated. Harold was to be the last English-speaking king for three hundred years. The Norman Conquest was rapid. Within five years of the Battle of Hastings, William had dispossessed nearly all important English landholders and granted their land to his followers.

The Normans who seized the estates of the Saxon nobles changed the landscape of England. Where the rambling wooden halls of the Saxon nobles had stood open to the peasants of the countryside, the Normans now built castles to dominate subjects hostile to their new lords. Built with forced Saxon labor, castles rose above the surrounding countryside on huge mounds of dirt surrounded by defensive earth walls and ringed by moats. The first castles were thrown up in haste and built of wood. In time the Normans cemented their hold on the country quite literally: they built castles of stone and mortar. These castles, so durable that many survive today, became the fixed points of power throughout England. By the end of the eleventh century, French-speaking Normans held all the important positions of power in England.

The Anglo-Saxons were reduced to the status of a servant people. They did the hard and underpaid work of the land: growing crops, grinding grain, spinning flax, shoeing horses, and hauling wood and stone to build the increasingly elaborate castles and estates of the Normans. Robin Hood, an actual person as well as a figure of lore, robbed the rich Norman overlords to share the wealth with the oppressed Saxons.

The Conquest Reshapes the Language:
From Bilingual to the Blending of French and English Vocabulary

The Normans spoke French, and the Latin roots of French were quite different from the Germanic roots of Anglo-Saxon. The Norse of the Danish Vikings had been a language some Anglo-Saxons could understand; the French of the Normans was not.

For two hundred years following the Norman conquest, two languages were spoken in England. The language of the ruling class was French; the language of the underclass was Anglo-Saxon, or English. That structure of power and class is reflected in the language we speak today. During the 1300s, English re-emerged as the primary language of England, but it was a changed English: it had lost many Anglo-Saxon words and gained many French ones. The new blend of vocabulary reflected the history that followed the Conquest. In the word lists below, notice that words of French origin are grouped by areas of life where the Normans were dominant following the conquest: military power, law and government, art, fashion, dining. Words of the Germanic origin reflect the life of the Anglo-Saxons as a peasant and laboring people: the seasons, the landscape, the marking of time, domestic animals, basic foods, family relationships, the world of the fisherman, the tools and materials of the worker.

Words of French origin

army	captain	government	defendant
navy	combat	state	judge
battle	beseige	royal	attorney
enemy	fortress	authority	jury
peace	dungeon	tax	evidence
defense	moat	revenue	verdict
soldier	tower	crime	fine
art	fashion	dinner	herb
painting	robe	feast	boil
sculpture	lace	beef	stew
beauty	jewel	veal	platter
color	satin	cream	table
music	fur	sugar	fruit
poem	diamond	salad	peach

Words of Anglo-Saxon origin

stars	storm	morning	cow
moon	hail	evening	sheep
sun	dew	day	goat
field	mist	night	bee
tree	snow	week	lamb
leaf	winter	month	calf
stone	summer	year	swine
meat	man	whale	rope
milk	wife	fish	hammer
salt	mother	boat	bench
water	father	sail	nail
wheat	child	sea	wheel
butter	brother	water	leather
honey	folk	ship	copper

The picture presented by these lists is oversimplified, of course. The influx of French vocabulary was a disorderly, human process and didn't always fit neatly into these categories.

Though French vocabulary replaced Anglo-Saxon vocabulary in many areas of the language, French did not replace it. Why? Why did the language of the peasants, rather than the language of the rulers, emerge as the common language of England? The reasons are many. The first is sheer numbers. Though the Normans held political power, they were a minority. Only one person out of ten in England was Norman. Norman lords had to learn the English of the peasants and servants in order to run their estates. Merchants who migrated from Normandy to England following the Conquest found they needed to learn the language if they wanted their business to thrive. When Normans intermarried with the English, as many did, the predominance of French was further undercut.

In addition, a series of historical events contributed to the decline of French and the revival of English. A major blow to the dominance of French occurred when King John of England lost Normandy to King Louis VII of France in 1204. Normans who held estates in both England and Normandy were forced to abandon one or the other. They had to choose which king they would serve and decide whether to be French or English. No longer could they shuttle back and forth as they pleased. The nobles who chose allegiance to England were cut off from the mainstream of French language and culture. They lost the closeties to the continent that kept a sense of French identity alive among them.

A further blow to the survival of French came when France and England fell into the prolonged period of fighting (1337-1453) known as the Hundred Years' War. Though many in the upper classes still spoke French, they had known no home but England for over a hundred years and considered themselves English. France was now the enemy. Thus the prestige of French declined and a sense of English nationalism grew.

Another major event of the 1300s, the Plague, contributed indirectly to the growing importance of English. The Plague struck England in 1349, killing forty percent of the population. In the resulting upheaval, social and economic barriers diminished. For Anglo-Saxons who survived the Plague, there were new opportunities. Because of the serious labor shortage, wages rose sharply. In the confusion of the times, many were able to break free of their legal bondage to one man's land and travel about, seeking the highest wage. Others migrated to the towns where the growth of trade and crafts supported a growing middle class, many of whom rose to positions of considerable wealth. Those who spoke English had increasing influence and power.

The revival of English was accompanied by a flowering of English literature, most notably the tales and poetry of Geoffrey Chaucer. Chaucer's language reflected the English that was becoming the language of the land—an English greatly enlarged by French vocabulary. Part of Chaucer's genius was to use the full range of the language that swirled around him—from its earthy Germanic core to the often musical and multisyllabic French words that had now given English a new look.

The Renaissance:
English Receives an Influx of Latin Words

Latin entered the English language through an invasion that was peaceful—the Renaissance of the 1500s. Latin had been the language of learning ever since the crumbling of the Roman Empire during the fifth century because Latin was the language of Christianity. Only under the protection of church monasteries did the arts of reading and writing survive the violence and upheaval that spread through Europe after the fall of the Roman Empire. For centuries, the only schools were church schools. When universities began to develop independently, Latin continued to be the language of learning.

Starting with the adoption of Christianity in England in 597, Latin words had trickled into the language through the church, its schools, and its influence on daily life: *altar, angel, candle, chalice, mass, priest, school, verse, meter, grammar, notary, lentil, millet, pear, radish, savory, lily, cap.* During the Renaissance, the trickle became a flood. Latin, accompanied by a comparatively smaller number of Greek words, flowed into English as the vocabulary of intellectual thought. A revival of learning led to the rediscovery of the classical writings of Greece and Rome. The Greek classics were first translated into Latin, then both were translated into English because of popular demand, demand created by the printing press. William Caxton had introduced the printing press to England in 1476 and by the mid-1500s books, pamphlets and single-sheet "broadsides" poured from the presses. The wealth of reading material inspired increasing numbers of people to learn to read. The literate public grew rapidly, further fueling the productivity of the publishers. A growing number of the works were by English authors and written in English. Authors who wrote in Latin might get rejection notices, such as the one received by Thomas Drant in 1567: "Though, sir, your book be wise and full of learning, yet peradventure it will not be so saleable." Classics previously published in Latin for a small band of Latin-speaking scholars were now translated into English for more profitable sales to the general public. One challenge in translating Latin into English was finding adequate vocabulary. Because Latin had been the language of scholarship, English lacked a vocabulary for expressing scholarly ideas. Many translators responded to the challenge by simply anglicizing Latin words—words intimately familiar to *them* because Latin was their second language. Because English already contained many French words, which are derived from Latin, the new vocabulary did not seem entirely strange to the general public either. Many of the new words passed quickly from books, where they first appeared, into general speech.

The invasion of Latin and Greek vocabulary was not entirely peaceful, however. Major arguments broke out over whether the new words enriched English or ruined it. Some writers got so carried away with using Latin words that their writing became overblown and difficult to understand. The growing number of "erudite" words brought into the language created barriers for those who knew no Latin. The following exchange between Groucho and Chico Marx might have come from this period:

> GROUCHO: If we're successful in disposing of these lots, I'll see that you get a nice commission.
>
> CHICO: What about some money?

Loud voices were raised against those who used "inkhorn terms," as many of the new words were called. Champions of "pure" English, in their attempt to purge the language of the growing Latin influence, proposed substitutes for the non-English impostors: *mooned* for *lunatic, gainrising* for *resurrection* and even *ungothroughsome* for *impenetrable.* Other writers eased Latin words into the language by pairing them with familiar synonyms, as did Sir Thomas Elyot: "*animate* or give courage," "*devulgate* or set forth," "*obfuscate* or hid," "*explicating* or unfolding." Shakespeare, of course, seized all the resources of the burgeoning language, celebrating both the earthy energy of "pure" English and the rolling syllables of Latin imports, sometimes setting "native" words beside the Latin to interpret them:

> Will all great Neptune's ocean wash this blood
> Clean from my hand? No; this my hand will rather
> The multitudinous seas incarnadine,
> Making the green one red.
>
> (*Macbeth*)

New words flooding into English during the Renaissance rose to a volume of 10,000-12,000, the great majority of them Latin. About 5,000 of those words remain in use today. Translations of classics were not the only source of new vocabulary. Activity in many fields spurred the growth of the language. Explorers set sail on voyages of discovery, centers of trade and commerce flourished and grew, new arts and technologies blossomed. Galileo explored mathematical and physical laws, as well as astronomy, William Harvey discovered circulation of the blood and William Gilbert was a pioneer in discovering magnetism. Latin and Greek provided *navigation, mathematics, circulation, skeleton, commerce, physics, gravity,* and *magnetism* (possible alternatives using non-classical sources would have been *course-charting, number-lore, blood-movement, bone-parts,* etc.). Here is a sampling of other Latin and Greek words that entered the language during that period: *scientific, thermometer, atmosphere, chronology, system, antithesis, heterodox, conjecture, expectation, conclusion, method, function, capacity, dexterity, democracy, politician, jurisprudence, audacious, egregious, malignant, compatible, conspicuous, appropriate, necessary, incredible, rational, intellect, genius, history, moderate, magnify, prosecute, indict, testify, notary, hereditary, popular, individual, habitual, private, solitary, spacious.*

English after the Renaissance

During the years that followed the Renaissance, the pace of change slowed. Publication of the first substantial English dictionary, Samuel Johnson's *Dictionary* (1775), was one reflection of a widespread impulse toward settling in to define "correct" English after the upheaval of the Renaissance. English continued to change, of course. New events generated new vocabulary and people continued to coin new words. However, the resources people used for creating new words did not change much after the Renaissance. The basic word stock we draw on today, as we combine and re-combine elements, was in place by then: a Germanic base joined with major strands of French and Latin vocabulary, as well as a small but significant strand of Greek vocabulary. For new scientific and scholarly terms, we still draw on Latin and Greek. Although English has continued to absorb foreign words—from British sailors and settlers who brought words home from all around the world, and from immigrants who have contributed words to American English—these borrowings have added threads of color to the language rather than giving it a look as radically new as those created first by the Norman Conquest and then by the Renaissance.

The Mixed Heritage of English:
Variety and Diversity in One Language

The mixed heritage of English provides great variety within one language. We have a vocabulary based on two sets of roots—a Germanic set familiar through the common names of things around us, and a Latin and Greek set often used for expressing abstract ideas. We have a language rich in synonyms and distinctly varied in its levels of formality. We also have a spelling system that gives many people a headache because it contains the different spelling patterns of several languages.

Two Sets of Roots: Familiar and Unfamiliar

Children learn the familiar names of things as a natural part of growing up, but learning names based on Greek and Latin roots often requires special effort. What is the *solar* system? A system that revolves around the sun. What is an *arboretum*? A *dormitory*? Young children know the words *sun*, *tree*, and *sleep*, but few know that the Latin roots *sol-*, *arbor-*, and *dorm-* also mean "sun," "tree," and "sleep." By contrast, a Spanish child is likely to know that the *systema solar* has something to do with the sun because the word for sun in Spanish is *sol*. In Spanish, complex vocabulary tends to be built on the words that children learn as they are growing up. In English, however, complex vocabulary is often built on roots that are different from those that underlie our everyday words. The adjective that describes "things having to do with dogs" is *canine*. The adjective that describes "things having to do with horses" is *equine*. The Latinate adjectives must be learned, not as extensions of the familiar names of the animals, but as separate vocabulary words.

English then is based on two sets of roots—familiar and unfamiliar. The familiar roots tend to be those of Germanic origin because, as we have seen, the Anglo-Saxon vocabulary that survived the Norman Conquest was the vocabulary of down-to-earth reality: *eat, sleep, wake, walk, run, come, go, bed, bowl, knife, roof, floor, room, rake, plow, seed, grain*. The words that survived in the speech of peasants living close to the land not only are familar, they often have an earthy liveliness as well: *creep, wriggle, sway, droop, slouch, crumple, shatter, flutter, rustle, ramble, hustle, fetch, fling, swoop, glide, glitter, blaze, dazzle, flash, flicker, dawdle, drift, ripple, splash, spray*. Our Germanic words are often the vivid words of the language.

61

The unfamiliar roots of the language are those of Latin and Greek origin. These roots underlie both the French words that came into the language following the Norman Conquest (French started off as "bad Latin," a provincial dialect of the Roman Empire) and the Latin and Greek vocabulary that entered English in the Renaissance. Words based on these roots are often less vivid for us because they are a step removed from our everyday names for things. Thus, *cordial*, based on the Latin *cor*, which means "heart," does not have the immediacy of the word *hearty*. (We do not always want a familiar immediacy, and at times prefer the more distant *cordial*.) Words based on the Greek *photo-* and *tele-* do not suggest images of light and distance as readily as vocabulary based on Germanic words of the same meaning, *light* and *far*. The word *retain*, based on the French form of the Latin *ten*, "to hold," does not have the same immediacy as the Germanic phrase "hold back."

To describe English as based on two sets of roots, familiar and unfamiliar, is, of course, to oversimplify. Many words of Latin origin, especially those that entered the language through French, became so integrated into daily speech that they are as familiar as any words in the language. The words *cry, touch, clear, mean, rude, cruel, calm*, and *safe*—all of French origin—have the same immediacy for us as words of Germanic origin. What remains true, however, is that many of the "big" words of the language are based on unfamiliar roots. The word *geography* is based on the Greek for "earth" (*ge*), not on the familiar word *earth*. In German, by contrast, the word for "geography" (*Erdkunde*) is built on the common word for "earth" (*Erde*). In German, as in the Romance languages, there often is continuity between common names and complex vocabulary. In English there seldom is.

Synonyms and Levels of Formality

Having a vocabulary drawn from several languages can create difficulties, but the mixed heritage of English also gives us a word stock rich in synonyms. Look at the following word pairs:

eat / dine	begin / commence
climb / ascend	rot / decay
teach / instruct	speed / velocity
smart / intelligent	grow / develop
dawdle / procrastinate	need / require
scold / reprimand	handle / manage

deadly / mortal	spit / expectorate
fix / repair	deep / profound
hurt / injure	hard / obdurate
end / terminate	light / illuminate

In each pair of synonyms the first word is of Germanic origin, the second of French or Latin origin. Each synonym covers a slightly different range of meaning, allowing us to draw fine distinctions that are not always possible in other languages. Sometimes the distinctions are connected to the degree of formality we associate with a word. The Latinate words usually have a more formal tone than their Germanic synonyms. We *eat* at McDonald's; we *dine* at an elegant restaurant. The government prefers the formality (and cushioning obscurity) of *terminating* a program to the informality (and frankness) of *ending* it. You and I may want to throw a little *light* on a subject; a philosopher might seek to *illuminate* it. English is full of synonyms that allow us to choose the tone and level of formality that best suit our purpose. It is the mixed heritage of English that gives us an abundance of synonyms and a vocabulary larger than that of any other Western language.

Phrases: Another Source of Synonyms

Synonyms can be phrases as well as words. We can *talk over* the day's events or *discuss* them, *come to* a conclusion or *arrive at* it. We can *let go* or *release, put off* or *postpone, set up* or *establish, try out* or *audition, give up* or *relinquish, put up with* or *tolerate, rise above* or *transcend, breathe in* or *inhale, run into* or *encounter, speak up for* or *advocate*. We coin phrases as readily as we coin words, and popular speech is full of them: *clam up, buzz off, space out, rip off, chill out*. The words in these phrases are assembled the way affixed words are assembled, but in a phrase the elements of meaning are left freestanding and in an affixed word they are "glued" together.

The use of phrases as alternatives to affixed words became prevalent in English because of changes in its Germanic vocabulary. If you look at the Lord's Prayer in Anglo-Saxon (below), you will see unfamiliar affixes attached to otherwise reasonably familiar words: the *-um* of *heofunum* (heaven), the *-a* of *willa* (will), the *ge-* of *gelaed*. Prior to the Norman Conquest, the Germanic vocabulary of English had many more affixes than are in active use today. Many affixes began to "fade," as linguists say, and fall out of use. The process began before the Conquest and continued for several hundred years. Some

Fæder ūre,

þū þe eart on heofonum,

sī þīn nama gehālgod.

Tōbecume þīn rīce

Gewurþe ðīn willa on eorðan swā swā on heofonum.

Ūrne gedæghwāmlīcan hlāf syle ūs tō dæg.

And forgyf ūs ūre gyltas, swā swā wē forgyfað ūrum gyltendum.

And ne gelǣd þū ūs on costnunge,

ac ālȳs ūs of yfele.   Sōþlīce.

(The Lord's Prayer in Anglo-Saxon)

affixes disappeared altogether: no words today begin or end with *ge-*, *-um*, or *-a*. Other affixes remain embedded in our vocabulary, but are no longer used to form new words: the *be-* of *behold, between, become,* and *because*; the *for-* of *forgive, forsake, forbid,* and *forget*; the *with-* of *withhold, withstand, without,* and *withdraw*.

As affixes were lost, the meaning was carried instead by freestanding words. For example, our tendency today is to put *hold* and *up* together in a phrase (*hold up*) rather than to combine them in an affixed word like *uphold*—a word that predates the Norman conquest. *Uphold, behold, withhold, withstand, understand, outstanding,* and *bystander* all reflect the earlier period when verbs were usually modified to express new meaning through affixing. Today, our tendency is to build a family of phrases on *hold* or *stand*, instead of a family of words: *hold up, hold off, hold down, hold onto, hold back, on hold,* and *stand by, stand for, stand up to, stand up for,* etc.

The "imported" Latinate words of the language did not undergo the same changes as the "native" Germanic words and remain highly affixed. Having both strands of vocabulary in the language often allows us a choice between a Germanic phrase and an affixed Latin word: we can *obtain* something or *get hold of* it, we can be *detained* on our way to a meeting or *held up*, we can *substitute* for others or *stand in* for them. The rhythm and feel of the phrase is different from the rhythm and feel of the affixed word. The choices we make as we use one or the other shape the style of our speaking and writing.

The Different Spelling Patterns of Several Languages Thrown Together

For a child who can sound out words, Spanish spelling is easy. It is almost always true that each sound can be represented by one, and only one, letter. The child who tries to spell English words by sounding them out, however, quickly runs into difficulties. If you rely solely on your ear when spelling *nation*, you are likely to spell it n-a-s-h-u-n. If you rely solely on your ear when spelling *school* and *night*, you are likely to spell them *s-k-o-o-l* and *n-i-t-e*. In English, any one sound may be represented by any of several letters, in part because the language includes spelling patterns from Anglo-Saxon, French, Latin, and Greek. Often, the spelling of a word is a clue to its identity. Here are a few of the clues.

Anglo-Saxon

Words of one and two syllables that begin with silent letters are usually of Anglo-Saxon origin. The letters were not always silent. In Anglo-Saxon times (known to linguists as the period of Old English) both of the beginning consonants in the following words were pronounced.

knee	gnaw	wrist
knob	gnarl	wrinkle
knuckle	gnat	wrench
knight	gnash	wrong

Words with *gh* are also of Anglo-Saxon origin. Though now silent, the *gh* was pronounced in Old English and Middle English (the English spoken in the Middle Ages following the Norman Conquest) with a guttural, throat-clearing sound similar to that given the *ch* in the German *nacht*.

fight	bought	caught
sight	thought	taught
high	ought	haughty
sigh	fought	naughty

A good way to help students remember these silent letters is to have them experiment with pronouncing the words as they were originally pronounced.

French

We can be fairly certain that a word entered the language via French when we encounter the following:

- Two-syllable words that end in *-ain*:

mountain	bargain	maintain
fountain	refrain	contain
certain	complain	obtain

- Words that end in *-ue*:

blue	hue	virtue
due	continue	statue
sue	value	revenue
glue	construe	retinue

- Words in which *ci* is pronounced like *sh*:

gracious	spacious	magician
delicious	special	suspicious
precious	musician	pernicious

Latin or French

Words ending in *-ture* or *-tion* are of French or Latin origin.

pasture	structure	nation	fraction
nature	armature	station	addition
capture	aperture	caption	subtraction
adventure	agriculture	election	selection
fracture	horticulture	mention	traction
culture	ligature	invention	eruption

Sometimes a Latin root, in passing through French, has acquired a distinctive French spelling. The French form of the Latin *cor-*, for example, is *cour-*, as in the word *courage*. The French form of the Latin *ten-* is *tain-*. The French form appears in the words *contain* and *retain*; the Latin form appears in the words *content* and *retention*. During the Renaissance the French spelling of many words was "corrected" to a Latin spelling by scholars who considered the classical languages to be the truest and purest form of language. Thus *parfait*, the French form of *perfect* found in the English of Chaucer's day, was "corrected" to *perfect*. Therefore, it is often difficult to tell whether a word originally came into English through French or through Latin.

Greek

You know a word is of Greek origin if it has a *ph* or if it has a *ch* that is pronounced with a *k* sound.

photograph	autograph	school	ache
phonograph	symphony	character	echo
physics	hyphen	Christmas	chaos
philosophy	atrophy	chorus	chrome
phobia	physical	chord	chlorine
phrase	telephone	choir	chronological

Words that begin with a silent *p* are of Greek origin. In Greek the *p* is still pronounced.

pneumonia	pterodactyl	ptolemy	psoriasis
pneumatic	ptomaine	pseudonym	psychology

Words with the consonant cluster *rh-* come from Greek:

rhetoric	rheumatism	rheostat
rhythm	hemorrhage	rhinoceros
rhubarb	rhapsody	

The story behind such "tricky" patterns—the story of the invasions that shaped English—can make some of the challenges of English spelling both interesting and understandable.

The Indo-European Family of Languages

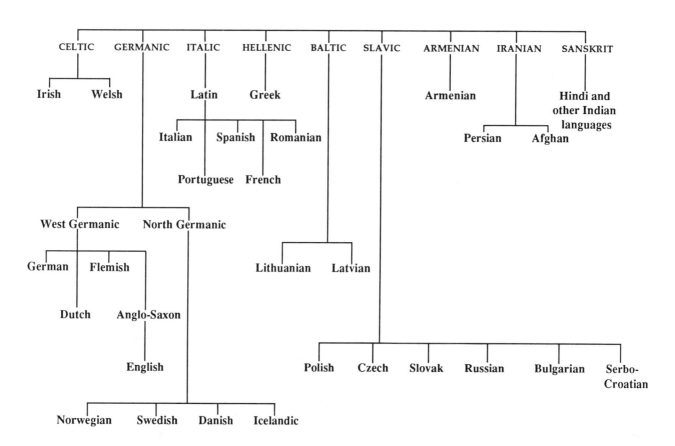

This is an abbreviated chart. A more complete chart can be found on the inside back cover of the 1969 edition of *The American Heritage Dictionary* and on pp. 112-113 of *The American Heritage Dictionary of Indo-European Roots* (1985).

Indo-European Origins:
The Languages That Contributed to English
Are Ultimately Related

The roots of words brought to England by the Normans reached back to Latin. The roots of words spoken by the Anglo-Saxons were of Germanic origin. Differences between these separate strands of language are many, but in the early nineteenth century linguists began tracing the separate strands back to a common source. Using word clues and clues of grammar, they discovered that, like most European languages, French and Anglo-Saxon share a common ancestor. Linguists named the ancestor Indo-European and pieced together clues that suggest that Indo-European was spoken about six or seven thousand years ago by tribes living in the area today known as southern Siberia. These tribes eventually began heading outward in all directions—some branching out across Europe, others migrating around the eastern edge of the Mediterranean and down into India. As the Indo-European tribes became isolated from one another, each followed its own separate path of change. From one common language, many separate languages evolved—all the languages pictured on the Indo-European chart.

The chart shows that some members of the Indo-European family are more closely related than others. You might say that Anglo-Saxon and German are siblings, but that Anglo-Saxon and French are cousins. English and Sanskrit are very distant cousins. Speaking of family connections, it should be noted that Indo-European is just one of many language families: Chinese belongs to the Sino-Tibetan family; the Cree language belongs to the Algonquin family; Arabic belongs to the Semitic family; Swahili belongs to the Bantu family.

Below are some of the word clues linguists used as they traced the Indo-European family tree and reconstructed its roots. Can you guess what English words belong in the blanks at the head of each column?

ENGLISH	_____	_____	_____
GERMAN	mutter	nacht	schnee
DUTCH	moeder	nacht	sneeuw
SWEDISH	mor	natt	sno
LATIN	mater	noct-	niv-
FRENCH	mère	nuit	neige
SPANISH	madre	noche	nieve
ITALIAN	madre	notte	neve
GREEK	meter	nukt-	nipha
RUSSIAN	mat	noch	sneg
SANSKRIT	mataram	naktam	snehas

Similarities can be seen fairly easily when these cognates (word relatives) of *mother, night,* and *snow* are assembled in one chart, but many other patterns of connections were not clear until linguists pieced them together. Through the common ancestry of Indo-European, then, the languages that contributed to English—Anglo-Saxon, Old Norse, French, Latin, and Greek—are all ultimately related. The few tribes who spoke the "parent" Indo-European tongue would be astonished to glance through history and see how their language has evolved.

American English: The Story Continues

The story of English continues to be one of change. In his book *Word Play*, Peter Farb tells of a young English woman who entered a convent in 1914 and remained in total seclusion for twenty-eight years. When she emerged, social customs and the map and politics of Europe were radically different, but what confused her most was the language people spoke. Words familiar to her had fallen out of use and many new expressions had come into being. Any person isolated for thirty years would have a similar problem of re-entry. Language is always changing. New experiences produce new vocabulary. The space age generated *astronaut, blast-off, lift-off, splashdown, boil-off, skylab*. Existing words took on new meaning: *docking, satellite, thrust, capsule, shuttle. In orbit* and *spaced out* became descriptions of psychological states. The term *spaceship earth* engendered a new perspective on the planet.

From the first days of settlement on the Atlantic coast, the American experience has shaped American English. Early settlers coined names for the features of the territory they pioneered: *foothill, bluff, hollow, water gap, backwoods, underbrush, watershed*. From contact with French and Spanish settlers came *prairie, bayou*, and *butte*, and *canyon, mesa*, and *arroyo*. As the country expanded into French and Spanish territories, local place names remained to remind us of their history: Baton Rouge, Louisiana, St. Louis, Sault Sainte Marie, Fond-du-Lac, Des Moines, Grand Teton; Nevada, Colorado, Rio Grande, San Antonio, El Paso, Orlando, Florida, California, San Diego, San Francisco. Names of New World plants and animals were adopted from Native American languages: *woodchuck, chipmunk, skunk, moose, opossum, hickory, pecan, persimmon, catalpa, hominy, squash*. Many place names are, of course, similarly drawn from American Indian languages: *Massachusetts, Connecticut, Minnesota, Mississippi, Tallahassee, Tuscaloosa, Roanoke, Potomac, Chesapeake, Susquehanna, Rappahannock, Passaic, Raritan, Penobscot, Kennebec, Merrimac*.

As farmers moved west, the challenge of putting new land to the plow produced the word *sodbusters*. From *cowboys* came *roundup* and *to bite the dust*. As rails were laid for a new form of transportation, the words *railroad, boxcar, switchyard*, and *cow catcher* (the front fender of the engine) were coined and *sidetrack, backtrack, make the grade, be in the clear*, and *reach the end of the line* quickly moved beyond the confines of the rails to express more general ideas. The Gold Rush gave us several metaphors that are still in the language: *pan out, stake a claim, strike it rich, hit pay dirt.* Clearing the land generated *bobsled* (usually two short, or "bobbed," sleds hitched together for carrying logs), *lumberjack,* and *fly off the handle*—as ax heads did with sometimes deadly results and as lumberjacks often did in the isolation of logging camps. Encounters with the weather inspired *blizzard* (probably of onomatopoeic origin), *cold-snap,* and *cloud-burst.* High spirits and a love of rolling sounds on the tongue gave birth to *rambunctious, scalawag, hornswoggle,* and *skedaddle.* One lure of the frontier was *lighting out* and leaving your troubles behind you. If you needed to leave town quickly, you could not only *scoot* or *skedaddle,* you could also *high tail it, hot foot it, pull stakes, make tracks, fly the coop,* or *hit the trail.*

If you were in the Ozarks you might *cut mud,* leave *lickety-whoop,* and *skin your eyes* (be alert) to make sure no one was following you. Many regions spawned their own turns of speech, which did not necessarily make it beyond the borders of the region. In the Ozarks you might also *raise sand* (create a disturbance), *cut your own weeds* (mind your own business), or *touch hands* with your neighbors (cooperate with them, stick together), while keeping your eye on the clouds to see if the coming rain is going to be a *drizzle-drozzle,* a *gully-washer,* a *fence-lifter,* a *goose-drowner,* or a *toad-strangler.* Along the Maine coast you might have to bring a sailboat to port by *ash breeze* (using oars) or you might be a *shorehugger* who never ventures far on a boat—or any other enterprise. You might feel that everything is *bung up and bilge free* (in good order, like casks properly stored on a boat) if you *get your bait back* (break even on a deal). If you do so well as to have a few dollars *salted down* (set aside for the future the way salted meats were stored on boats and in lumber camps), you might get *all rigged out* (dressed up) to celebrate. In the West you might encounter an *Arizona cloudburst* (sandstorm), take the *ankle express* (go by foot), or feel *cold-footed* (cowardly) when tangling with a *barb wire deal* (tough situation to handle) or with someone who is *all horns and rattles* (in a fit of temper—like a cow aiming its horns and a snake shaking its rattles.)

Just as regional speech often reflected regional particularities, activities shared by people across the country created a shared vocabulary. American politics, springing from new experiments in government, had a flavor and a vocabulary all its own. In the late 1800s the use of barns for performances by itinerant actors came to be known as *barnstorming*, a word soon borrowed by equally itinerant politicians—as was the *bandwagon* of the circus parade. *Grandstanding* (borrowed from baseball) politicians often seized the attention of voters with lively turns of speech: *landslide, gag rule, dark horse, gerrymander, lobbyist, pork barrel, lame duck, fat cat.* Sports and games contributed many figures of speech to the language: *out in left field, off base, play hardball, back a winner, on the ropes, saved by the bell, cut a deal, ante up, in the chips, cash in, par for the course.* With the advent of electricity we could get a *charge* out of things and with the advent of cars we could *step on it* or be *out of gas.* Aviation gave us *on the beam, flying blind, tailspin, nose dive,* and *bail out.* American coinages have often been graphic and lively: *fork over, cave in, go-getter, ripsnorter, roughneck, back talk, scofflaw, has-been, do-gooder, down and out, flat-footed, roughhouse, comeback, get a move on, make good, no slouch, backbone, start off, show up, stay put, cut and run, sit up and take notice.*

Immigrants brought words of diverse origins into American English. From French settlers in the Louisiana territory came *levee, depot, bureau,* and *picayune* (derived from the name of a small French coin.) From Spanish-speaking immigrants came the words *mustang, lasso, lariat, bronco, pinto, corral, stampede, rodeo, ranch, adobe, siesta, patio, bonanza, tornado, tortilla, tacos, tamale, chili,* and *cafeteria.* From German settlers came *cookbook, delicatessen, kindergarten,* and *hoodlum,* and the expressions *and how, no way, will do* (direct translations from German). Speakers of Yiddish have given us *kibbitzer, klutz, chutzpah, mensch, schlep, schmaltz,* and *schmooze.* The vocabulary of many nations is especially evident in the foods that immigrant groups have contributed to the American diet: *sauerkraut, pumpernickel, hamburger, frankfurter, liverwurst,* and *schnitzel* (German); *blintzes, borscht, matzoh, bagels,* and *lox* (Yiddish); *kielbasa* (Polish); *parmesan, pasta, spaghetti, macaroni, salami, ravioli, minestrone, pizza, zucchini,* and *broccoli* (Italian); *lutefisk* and *smorgasbord* (Scandinavian); *chop suey, chow mein, dim sum, soy* sauce, and *ketchup* (Chinese); *pita, humus,* and *tahini* (Middle Eastern); *goulash* and *paprika* (Hungarian); *yam, gumbo,* and *okra* (African).

African-Americans have made numerous contributions to American speech, contributions that go beyond individual words of African origin, such as *tote, juke* (in jukebox), *jazz*, and *banjo*. Jazz, that unique contribution of African-Americans to American and world culture, was but one territory where they defined the vocabulary: *jam, riff, in the groove, cat, mellow, bop, hip.* Improvisation, which lies at the heart of jazz, is central not only to African musical tradition, but also to the spoken traditions of the griots, or African bards.[1] Forbidden to learn to read and write well after their arrival in the United States, African-Americans preserved elements of their oral traditions in various forms. Rap songs, hip-hop, playing the dozens, and pulpit oratory, diverse though they be, all share roots in African tradition through their emphasis on verbal agility and on the ability to compose during performance. It is interesting to note that Martin Luther King improvised the famous lines of his "I Have a Dream" speech. Reared in the African-American preaching tradition, King was a master of improvisation in rhythms and cadences familiar to African-American congregations but new to most of the nationwide audience who first heard them during the 1963 March on Washington. King had prepared a restrained, low-key speech for that occasion, but as he neared the end of it, he abandoned his text. As one author put it, he achieved permanent status as an American orator and statesman by "setting aside his text to cut loose and jam, as he did regularly from two hundred podiums a year."[2] In wholly different settings and often serving very different ends, rap artists and other street-corner poets in the inner city still practice a similar art of improvising.

The verbal inventiveness of such traditions has infused American popular speech with new terms, especially in recent years. The expressions *hang-up,*

---

[1] The bardic tradition, with its emphasis on spoken art and composition during performance, is of course a part of Western tradition as well. Both Homer and the Beowulf poet embody this tradition. Their bardic performances were written down—and thus preserved for us—as their civilizations were turning toward literacy. Alfred Lord's *The Singer of Tales* (Cambridge, Massachusetts: Harvard University Press, 1960) analyzes the elements of bardic performance using recorded interviews done in the 1930s (by Bela Bartok, among others) with Serbo–Croatian bards in Yugoslavia. These bards were still reciting epics as long as *The Iliad*—but they were the last generation to keep the art alive. Isidore Okpewho makes a similar analysis of bardic tradition in Africa in *The Epic in Africa: Toward a Poetics of Oral Performance* (New York: Columbia University Press, 1979). Because in the West emphasis on oral performance was displaced so long ago by emphasis on literary composition (the Yugoslavian bards were part of an Islamic tradition unfamiliar to most Westerners), our most direct link to that tradition runs through African-American heritage. Oral performance remained alive in Ireland much longer than it did in England or continental Europe and the rhythms of that tradition have influenced English literature. (Listen to Yeats "sing" his poetry.)

[2] Taylor Branch, *Parting the Waters* (New York: Simon and Schuster, 1988), p. 887.

rip off, uptight, make it, drop out, get it together, cool it, and *chill out* have, at various times, gained fairly wide currency. Current expressions coined by young African-Americans often spread worldwide, thanks to the popularity of their music and to global telecommunications. A production assistant for the PBS television series *The Story of English* was amazed to discover, as she watched the rough cut for the program on black English, that the latest expressions from Philadelphia's inner city were already on the tongue of her ten-year-old son in London.

Today English is spoken throughout the world. Movies, television, tapes, and other forms of technology create a pool of common experience among the various "Englishes"—British, American, Canadian, Indian, Australian, West Indian—but speakers in each setting adapt the language to their own situations. In India, many daily newspapers are published in English, but native words mix with English vocabulary in journalists' reports. In the West Indies, African patterns of pronunciation and grammar have shaped the native Creole and are influencing the "standard" English spoken in the islands, as well. Wherever English takes root, it comes to reflect the lives of those who speak it. In the words of Ralph Waldo Emerson, "Language is a city, to the building of which every human being [brings] a stone."

Linguistic Background

As you explore each word family, you will find that some changes in sounds and letters took place as the family developed. The brief explanations of such changes given in the word family chapters are sufficient for your students, but for those of you who would like further background, we include here a discussion of the following: why several of the Indo-European roots have unfamiliar consonant-*h* patterns; why knowing the history of silent letters can be helpful; why the vowels change from one word to another in a family; why *r* often shifts its position in a word; and why certain consonant shifts have been common in English and its parent languages. To bring some of this seemingly esoteric information down to earth, listen to some toddlers who are learning to speak. Does the toddler's version of a word have the same vowels as the version used by older members of the family? Do you hear *t*'s that are pronounced as *d*'s or *p*'s that are pronounced as *b*'s? Vowel shifts and consonant shifts are part of our personal history, as well as part of the history of the language.

Unfamiliar Consonant-*h* Patterns of Indo-European Roots

Why do the roots BHEL, DHREU, GHEIS, MEDHYO, and GHEL have consonant-*h* patterns that no longer exist in the English derivatives? The *h* in these roots represented a puff of breath following the consonants—a pronunciation unfamiliar to speakers of English. Just as people stopped pronouncing the sound represented by the *k* of *knee* and the *w* of *wrong*, they also stopped pronouncing the sound represented by the *h* in BHEL, DHREU, GHEIS, MEDHYO, and GHEL. Don't worry about how to pronounce these roots. You can pronounce them as though the *h* were silent, or you can make up your own version of a breathy sound. No one knows for sure how the *h* was pronounced.

We considered converting BHEL, DHREU, MEDHYO, and GHEL to Germanic forms that would eliminate the *h*, but decided against it because we found that students enjoy the air of mystery—the sense of connection with something ancient and different—of these exotic patterns. You may want to point out the Indo-European languages where such patterns still persist: Afghani, Hindu, and other Indian languages. The name Afghanistan, of course, is one example, and a map of Afghanistan provides others: Ghazni, Ghurian, Balkh, and Andkhvoy. Bhaktapur, Dhankuta, Junagadh, Mhow, Khandwa, Jhunjhunu, and Dharmsala are examples from India. The languages of Pakistan and Iran are also Indo-European in origin. In Pakistan you will find Jhal, Musa Khel, Bhera, and Dera Ghazi Khan, and in Iran Khorramabad, Sarakhs, Maragheh, and Abhar. In Greece, as well, you will find Khania, Khios, Dhomokos, Edhessa, and Khranidhion. If you know native speakers of any of these languages, you might ask them how the patterns are pronounced in their language. Names in the news and words imported from these regions (Khomeini, Bhutto, ghee, dharma, Buddha) can also point up the linguistic kinship of these other languages with Indo-European roots.

Silent Letters

When sounds fall silent, the letters that represent them are not always dropped. We no longer pronounce the *g* of *gnaw*, the *b* of *thumb*, the *l* of *walk*, the *t* of *fasten*, the *n* of *autumn,* or the *p* of *psychology.* The letters remain as clues to sounds that were once a part of the word—as the *h* of BHEL reminds us of a sound from the ancestry of English. The WER family (*wrap, wrestle, wriggle*, etc.), the GHEIS family (*ghost, ghastly, aghast*) and the GHEL, DHREU, MEDHYO, and GHEL roots all provide opportunities for alerting students to the idea that history lurks in silent letters. No letters started off as silent. Experimenting with sounding silent letters gives students an amusing way of remembering them.

Regional and cultural variations in pronunciation show that sounds that are enunciated in one area may be dropped in another. In Appalachian English, the *g* of the *ing* suffix is regularly dropped, and *lovin'* rhymes with *oven.* In Black English, final blends are regularly simplified, with only one of the letters pronounced: *child* becomes *chile, first* becomes *firs, send* becomes *sen.* In songs, *wild* is rhymed with *smile, when* rhymed with *friend.* Poetry and songs are always good clues to pronunciation. For instance, you can learn a lot about Elizabethan pronunciation by examining Shakespeare's rhymes. Be alert to patterns of pronunciation in your own classroom. If students have difficulty with spelling, they may find it helpful to know what letters are silent for them and need extra attention.

Vowel changes

Try the following exercise: run through the sounds represented by consonants, then pronounce sounds represented by vowels. Remember, you are pronouncing the sound represented by a letter, not the name of the letter.

Consonants

Notice that all of the consonant sounds involve cutting or filtering the flow of air that you exhale as you speak. When you pronounce the sounds represented by *d* or *t*, the air is cut by the tongue hitting the roof of the mouth. The air is filtered through closed teeth when you pronounce the sound represented by *s*. Linguists call such filtered sounds *fricatives* (a term related to the word *friction*). A fricative is formed when air is forced into a channel so narrow that hissing or buzzing results. Observe how you form other consonant sounds. Where in your mouth and with what (lips, tongue, teeth) do you form other consonant sounds?

Vowels

Notice the openness of vowel sounds. In pronouncing them you shape the air, but you do not cut or filter it. Because vowel sounds are more open (less clearly tied to a particular point of articulation—lips, tongue, teeth), they change form more readily. Listen to people whose accent is different than yours. How does it differ? Primarily in the vowel sounds. A northerner pronounces the number following nine as *ten*, but many southerners pronounce it as *tin*. Some New Englanders pronounce *ate* as though it were *et*. In these variations the consonant sounds remain the same and the vowel sound changes. Consonant sounds do change, but not as readily.

R as a Semi-vowel

Moving from the root WER to its derivatives *wrap, wreath,* etc., the pattern changes from *w*-vowel-*r* to *w*-*r*-vowel. This inversion of *r* and the vowel is common, both in the historical development of words and in some children's spelling. You may have taught children who, in spite of genuine attempts to learn the correct spelling, persist in spelling *birth* as *brith* or *scratch* as *scartch*. Such inversions occur relatively often because *r* is a semi-vowel.

Try pronouncing *birth* and *scratch.* Notice how you shape the sound represented by *r.* You "squeeze" the flow of air more tightly than you do when shaping vowel sounds, but you don't cut or filter the flow as you do when shaping sounds represented by such consonants as *b* or *f.* The *r* sound is not open enough to substitute for a vowel, but it is open enough to share with vowels a tendency toward shifting about.

It is not unusual, then, to find inversion represented by the shift from the vowel-*r* pattern of WER to the *r*-vowel pattern of *wrestle.* Children who have difficulty pinning an *r* to its proper position in a word will find comfort in knowing that people have been inverting *r*'s and vowels for centuries. Sometimes the knowledge cheers them enough so they are ready to tackle this spelling problem with renewed energy.

In spoken English, *r* sometimes slides out of the picture altogether. In some regions an *r* that follows a vowel tends to be lost and replaced by an *uh*-like vowel. Listen to politicians who have a Boston accent. They speak, not about the *future* of the country, but about its *fuchuh.* In some southern areas, *storage* is pronounced as *sto'age* and *barrel* as *b'al.* Listen to the various patterns of pronunciation in your classroom. Children who come from areas where *r* is not always pronounced may find it useful to recognize that, for them, *r* is sometimes a silent letter and may need extra attention when it crops up in the spelling of a word.

Consonant Shifts

Although consonant sounds are more stable than vowel sounds, they do sometimes change. Certain shifts are common in English and its parent languages. In the DWO and DERU families, the *d*-sound of the root and its Latin derivatives has shifted to the *t*-sound of the Germanic words of the family. The Latinate words of the DWO family are *double, duplicate, duplicity, deuce,* and *duet*; the Germanic words are *two, twelve, twenty, twice, twin, twine, twig, between,* and *twilight.* The Latinate words of the DERU family are *endure, obdurate,* and *duress*; the Germanic words are *trust, true, truce, tryst, tree, tray,* and *trough.*

How did the shift from *d* to *t* take place? Experimenting with how we make the sounds reveals that we form both of them with the same "mouth action": the tip of the tongue hits the roof of the mouth just behind the teeth. The

79

difference between the two is that the sound represented by *d* (/*d*/) is voiced and the sound represented by *t* (/t/) is unvoiced. Try making both sounds (be sure not to add a vowel sound after the /t/) while holding your throat. You will feel your vocal chords vibrate as you sound /*d*/, but not as you say /t/. A speech sound that involves vibrating the vocal chords is *voiced*; one that is made simply by cutting the flow of air, with no vibration of the vocal chords, is *unvoiced*. In English there are several pairs of consonant sounds in which one is a voiced or unvoiced version of the other: /*b*/ is a voiced /*p*/, /*g*/ is a voiced /*k*/, /*v*/ is a voiced /*f*/, and /*z*/ is a voiced /*s*/. The *th-* sound can either be unvoiced, as in *bath,* or voiced, as in *bathe.* All of these pairs have the same "mouth action" and differ only in terms of being voiced or unvoiced. We sometimes slip from one member of a pair to the other without realizing it. Shifting between /*d*/ and /t/ is particularly common. *Little* is often pronounced as though it were spelled *liddle. Walked, helped,* and *laughed* are regularly pronounced as though they were spelled *walkt, helpt,* and *laught.* Pronunciation is influenced by the sounds surrounding the /*d*/ or /t/ and by what feels "natural."

Both the KER and KEL families reflect a similar shift from the voiced /*g*/ to the unvoiced /*k*/. The original Indo-European form of KER is GER and the original Indo-European form of KEL is GEL. In this book, we have adapted the roots to their Germanic form to simplify exploration of vocabulary that had only the Germanic *k*-sound.

Some consonant shifts involve changes other than moving from a voiced to an unvoiced speech sound. The shift from /*k*/ to /*h*/ in the KERD/HEART and KAPUT/HEAD families is a shift from one unvoiced consonant to another. In this shift it is the "mouth action" that changes. Try making both sounds. You will notice that, as you make the *k*-sound, the back of your tongue hits the back of the roof of your mouth. When you make the *h*-sound the "mouth action" is focused in the same area, but the tongue drops down to squeeze—rather than to cut—the flow of air. (The relatively "open" sound represented by *h* makes it, like *r*, a semi-vowel. This is why, historically, it has been considered correct to use *an* rather than *a* before words beginning with *h*.) As in the shift from /*k*/ to /*h*/, most consonant shifts take place in the same region of the mouth, and it is relatively easy to imagine people moving from one point of articulation to the other.

A Word of Explanation about the Roots Used in *Origins*

The roots listed as the sources of word families in *Origins* have been drawn from *The American Heritage Dictionary of Indo-European Roots*. In the word family chapters, we do not identify the roots as Indo-European because we choose to focus on how they were used to create new words, not on labeling them.

For those of you who want to look up the roots in the *Dictionary*, a word of explanation is in order: these roots are not all presented in exactly the same form as they appear in the *Dictionary* (or the *Appendix* of the 1969 edition of *The American Heritage Dictionary*). In consultation with Calvert Watkins, the editor of the *Dictionary*, we made a few changes designed to make the material more accessible to students. In three cases roots are given in Germanic, rather than Indo-European form: FLEU is the Germanic form of the Indo-European PLEU; KEL is the Germanic form of the Indo-European GEL; and KER is the Germanic form of GER. In addition, we have given the root meanings of FLEU and KER in terms that are easier for elementary students to understand than those used in the *Dictionary*.

In the *Dictionary* you will often find roots that are spelled the same but have different meanings (as in bear, "to carry," and bear, the animal) and these are differentiated by numbers: BHEL¹, BHEL², etc. For the sake of simplicity, we do not use these numbers in *Origins*, but here are identifying numbers in case you are interested: BHEL², GER³ (KER), GHEL², GEL¹ (KEL), WER³.

Additional Word Families
Based on Indo-European Roots

Here are some additional word families based on Indo-European roots. Many are small and are fun to share informally during a spare moment or as a word or image of the family may arise. Others merit more attention. See the "Developing Your Own Word Families" section of the "Using *Origins*" chapter for ideas on exploring the larger families.

Like the word families of Volume 2, the following word families have been drawn from *The American Heritage Dictionary of Indo-European Roots* edited by Calvert Watkins (Boston: Houghton Mifflin, 1985). In some cases, roots that have different meanings are spelled the same, just as *mail* (armor) and *mail* (letters) have the same spelling but are unrelated. When this happens, roots are identified by numbers (as in BHEL[3] or MEL[8]).

Abbreviations indicating origins of words are as follows: *G* for Germanic, *L* for Latin, *F* for French, *Gk* for Greek, *It* for Italian, *R* for Russian, and *C* for Celtic.

ANGH. Tight, painfully constructed

> G. anger   L. anxiety, anxious
>   angst   anguish

ANK. To bend

> G. ankle   Gk. anchor
> L. angle

BABA. (A root that imitates indistinct or unarticulated speech.)

> G. baby, babe   It. bambino   F. baboon
>   babble   R. babushka   Gk. barbarian, barbaric

BHEL.[3] To thrive, bloom

G. blow (to flower)	L. flower	florist
bloom	flour	foliage
blossom	flourish	defoliate
blade	floral	portfolio

The transformation of the *b* of the Indo-European root to the *f* of its Latin derivatives is common, exemplified in this family and the following two families, as well as in the related words *brother* and *fraternal*, which both come from the Indo-European BHRATER. You may want to have students experiment with pronouncing both consonants to see how the "mouth action" involved takes place in the same area.

Blade originally referred to a blade of grass or similar plant and later by analogy of shape to part of a knife or sword. *Flour* was not originally distinguished from *flower* in its spelling. It originated in the phrases *flower of wheat, flower of barley, flower of meal*—meaning the finest portion of the grain—and only later came to have its own spelling and identity. The *folio* of *portfolio* is the Latin word for "leaf"—as in *leafing* through a book.

BHREG. To break

G. break	L. fracture
breach	fraction
	fragment
	fragile
	refract

BHREU. To boil, bubble, effervesce
The unifying idea is that of coming to life through bubbling, expanding, warming.

G. brew	F. ferment
broth	fervent
bread	effervescent
breath	
brood, breed	

DEL. Long   Later form: DHLON-GO

> G. long   L. longitude
>   length   longevity
>   linger   prolong
>   Lent   elongate

Lent comes from an Old English word for spring, which in turn comes from a Germanic word meaning "lengthening day."

DHER. To make muddy; darkness

> G. dark
>   dregs
>   dross

DHWER. Doorway—originally designating the entrance to the enclosure surrounding the house proper

> G. door   L. foreign
>   forest
>   forum

Foreign and *forest* both originally meant "outside or beyond the doors." A *forum* was originally the enclosed place around a home—a place "within the doors" or gates—and later a marketplace.

DRAGH. To draw (pull), drag on the ground

> G. draw   L. trail   detract
>   drawer   train   distract
>   drawback   tractor   extract
>   withdraw   tractable   retract
>   drawl   traction   subtract
>   drag   abstract
>   dragnet   attract
>   bedraggle   contract
>   draft
>   drink
>   drench

If you present this family to students, it might be better to give the root meaning as *pull*, since most students think of *draw* in terms of "drawing a picture" rather than in terms of its primary meaning of "pull" or "drag." *Drink* and *drench* may seem like odd members of the family. They are based on the imagery of drawing water in.

ED. To eat

      G. eat   L. edible
            etch

GEL. Cold; to freeze

      G. chill   L. gelatin
           cool   jelly
           cold   congeal
                      glacier

GEN. To compress into a ball

      G. knapsack   knoll   knead
           knob   knot   knock
           knuckle   knit   knell

Knit comes from origins meaning "to tie into a knot" and *knell* from origins meaning "to strike, as with a knobby object." All the *k*'s were once pronounced, of course. *Knife* is also a member of this family. A *knife* might have originally been a blunt instrument.

GENE. To give birth, beget

      G. kin   L. generate   ingenious   gentleman
           kind   generation engine   gentle
           kindred   engender   genes   generous
           kinship   progeny   genus   degenerate
           king   genesis   generic   genial
                          genius   gentry   congenial

GHER. To enclose

G. gird   L. orchard
    girdle   horticulture
    girth
    garden
    yard
    kindergarten

GHRE. To grow, become green

G. green   grass
    grow   graze

GNO. To know

G. know   L. notice   F. connoisseur
    can   notify
    canny   notorious   Gk. prognosis
    uncanny   notion   diagnosis
    cunning   noble   gnostic
    ken   ignoble
             cognitive
             cognizant
             ignore
             ignorant
             recognize

KAN. To sing

G. hen   L. chant   incantation
           enchant   cantor
           canticle charm

KEL. To cover, conceal

G. hall   L. color
    hull   cell

hole   conceal
hell
hollow
holster
helmet

Color comes from "that which covers" and *cell* from a word that meant storeroom or chamber.

KERS. To run

L. car	L. corridor	F. course
carry	current	
cargo	excursion	
career	occur	
	recur	
	cursory	

LEIS. Track, furrow

G. last (endure)	L. delirium
last (re: shoe)	
learn	
lore	

The metaphors here are intriguing. *Last* (to endure) comes from a word meaning "to follow a track"—and obviously comes from a time when following a track through the wilds was no easy matter. *Learning*, likewise, originates in the idea of following a track or course. *Lore* is the result of following such a path. *Delirium* comes from intermediate roots meaning "to go out of the furrow"— a metaphor from an agricultural society. *Last* (as in the *last* of a shoe) is the one obvious connection with the idea of a track or footprint.

LENTO. Flexible

G. lithe	L. relent
linden	lenient

LUFTUZ. Sky

    G. loft
       lift
       aloft

MEL[1]. Soft

G. melt	L. mollify	F. enamel
mild	emollient	
smelt	mollusk	

MEL[8]. To crush, grind

G. meal (coarsely ground grain)	L. mallet
mill, miller	malleable
millet	molar

The *meal* of this family is the *meal* of *cornmeal* or *oatmeal*. *Meal* (breakfast, lunch, etc.) comes from a root that means "a measure, mark or an appointed time".

MORI. Body of water

G. mere	L. marine	F. morass
marsh	submarine	
mermaid	marina	
	mariner	
	marinate	

MUS. A mouse, muscle (because of the resemblance of a flexing muscle to the movement of a mouse)

G. mouse	L. muscle

PED. Foot

G.		L.	
	foot		pedal
	fetter		pedestrian
	fetch		piedmont
	fetlock		podium
			expedite
			impede
			centipede

REUD. Red, ruddy

G.		L.	
	red		rouge
	ruddy		ruby
	rust		russet

SED. To sit

G.		L.	
	sit		sedentary
	set		sedate
	seat		sediment
	settle		assiduous
	saddle		dissident
	soot		reside
			subside

SKEI. To gleam

G.		L.	
	shine		scintillate
	shimmer		stencil
			tinsel

SKER. To cut

G.			L.		
	sharp	skirt		scrutiny	scribe
	shear, shears	skirmish		inscrutable	scribble
	shred	scrap		curt	script
	shrub	scrape		curtail	describe
	shirt	scrub			inscribe

short	scroll		prescribe
share			subscribe
shard			transcribe
shrew			manuscript
shrewd			

The *scribe* and *script* words have their origins in a root that means "to cut" because writing was first done by cutting into a surface with a sharp tool. There are also many words and phrases built on *cut*: *shortcut, undercut, cutback, cut in, cut off, cut out, cut loose, cut to the bone,* etc.

STA. To stand

G. stand	L. stable	standard	establish
stay	stage	stamen	restore
stem	statue	stamina	obstacle
stool	stature	staunch	substitute
steady	status	stanch	constant
steadfast	station	obstinate	destitute
homestead			circumstance
stalwart			

There are also many words and phrases built on *stand: bystander, outstanding, understand, stand for, stand up for, standby, stand-off, standoffish, stand-in, stand in for, stand up, stand up to, standpoint, standstill.*

STER. Stiff

G. stare
stark
starch
stern
stork
strut
startle

A *stare* is stiffer than a gaze, no?

90

TWER. To turn, whirl

G. storm L. turbine F. trouble
stir disturb
perturb

WE. To blow

G. weather L. vent, ventilate
wind
window
wing

A *window* was originally the "wind's eye."

WEBH. To weave

G. weave
web
waffle
woof, weft
wobble
wave (of the hand)
wave (of water)
waver

Body Metaphors in English

Head

headstrong
head of (a company, a country)
head up (a committee, etc.)
heading
headline
hard-headed
cool-headed

clear-headed
soft-headed
level-headed
muddle-headed
over one's head
to hold one's head high (to be proud)

Heart

hearty
heartless
open-hearted
heavy-hearted

heart-broken
warm-hearted
light-hearted
at the heart of (a city, etc.)

Face

two-faced
to save face

Nose

nosy
to look down one's nose at (someone, etc.)
to turn up one's nose

Eyes

to see eye to eye
to turn a blind eye to (something, etc.)
to shut your eyes to (something)

Ears

to turn a deaf ear to (someone, etc.)
to lend an ear
to be all ears

Shoulder

to shoulder a burden
shoulder to shoulder (united)

Back

to turn one's back on
behind one's back
off one's back

Arm

to keep at arm's length
to twist one's arm
to strong-arm

Hand

to handle
to have a hand in
to sit on one's hands
to dirty one's hands
(to be or to have) on hand
to set one's hand to; to turn one's hand to (something)
to hand over
to keep hands off

Knuckle

to knuckle under
to knuckle down

Foot

to put one's foot down
to get cold feet
to drag one's feet
to get one's feet wet
to keep one's feet on the ground
to stand on one's own two feet

Exploring Popular Speech

The material presented here came from a group of Washington, D.C., teachers during a workshop. The meanings given are approximate, since many of the terms can be fully understood only in context.

Term	Meaning	Probable Image
Solid	Expression of confirmation that can range from "okay" to "terrific"	Doesn't fall apart, holds together; can be relied on
Split	Leave	Image of separation
Out of it	Not in touch with what's going on	Spatial image—you're out on the periphery, not at the center
Spaced	Not at all in touch with what's going on	Into outer space. Compare the contrasting imagery of "down to earth."
Out to lunch Lunch box He's with the lunch bunch. He's lunchin'.	Not in touch with what's going on	Absence from the scene where business is being conducted
Laid back	Relaxed about things	The body at rest

Term	Meaning	Probable Image
Bent out of shape	In some kind of emotional pain or discomfort. Alternatively, being off balance psychologically, not having your act together.	Contorted body. If your body is bent out of its natural shape, you may be in pain or discomfort. Alternatively, if your body is bent out of shape, you're not in a position to perform smoothly.
Don't get your hips on your shoulders. Don't get hipped.	Same as above	Same as above
Nose out of joint	In a bad temper—with a sense of being put upon	A face reflecting unhappiness. Most adults have lost the facial mobil ity necessary for demon strating the expression well—children are best at it.
The hawk is out.	It's freezing cold.	Image of being gripped, seized by the cold. Compare "The cold held them in its grip" or "It's biting cold."
The eagle flies today.	It's payday.	From the image of the eagle on the dollar bill
Foxy	Beautiful, moves with elegance, sometimes sly	The animal and its characteristics

Some of the terms listed by the workshop group fell in a special category: the use of negative words to denote positive qualities, a use common in several West African languages and in African-American idiom. Thus, mean and bad denote "fine, super, excellent," and rags means "fancy clothes."

Sound Families

The following word clusters are linked through shared imagery and sound patterns. It should be emphasized here, as it was earlier, that the connection between the sound pattern—the initial consonant cluster—and the imagery is not an absolute one. Other sounds in a word or a definition that move a word clearly in another direction can override our tendency to associate a given sound pattern with particular imagery, experience, or feeling. Nevertheless, as the following word clusters or "sound families" demonstrate, the psychological tendency to associate sound and meaning has a firm base in reality. The sound families listed below are not, of course, definitive. We list the most obvious candidates for inclusion. You may find, as we do, that once you become alert to the link between *SW-* and the imagery of bending and turning, for example, you begin to see elements of these curvilinear movements in *SW-* words other than those listed below.

SW-. Associated with turning, bending

sweep	swing	sway	swirl
swoop	swerve	swivel	

Swoop and *swivel* actually come from an Indo-European root SWEI, which means to bend or turn. Two other words, *swift* and *swap*, come from the same root. The way they share in the imagery of bending and turning is not as immediately obvious, but can be fun to explore (compare the idea of *swapping* with the idea of "your turn"). Students often propose the words *swish, swoop,* and *swipe* as members of the sound family, as well. Although bending and turning movements are not explicit in the definitions of these words, the actions they describe often include elements of bending and turning.

SP-. Associated with movement outward—often a quick burst of movement

spit	spatter	spigot	sprinkle
spew	spurt	spray	spring
spout	spurn	sprawl	sprout
sputter	spume	spread	splash
			splatter

Spit, spew, spout, and *sputter* come from the Indo-European SPYEU, an expressive root meaning "to spew, to spit." The other words share in the expressive force that is grounded in the physical spitting forth of the *sp-* sound.

FL-. Associated with free, often quick, movement

flash	flicker	flap	flail
flare	flick	flip-flop	fling
flame	flip	flounce	

These words are in addition to all the members of the FLEU family.

A few other words participate in the sense of free movement associated with these words: *flamboyant, flag* (as in a flag waving in the breeze), and *flourish* (as in to pull something forth with a *flourish*).

SN-. Associated with the nose

snore	sneeze	sneer	snooty
sniff	snooze	snob	snotty
sniffle	snorkel	snicker	snout
snarl	snoot	snuff	
snort	snoopy	snuffle	

Snout, snuffle, snivel, sniff, snoop, and *snub* are all presented in *The Dictionary of Indo-European Roots* as coming from SNU, described as the "imitative beginning of Germanic words connected with the nose." The other words of the group participate in the connection between the *sn-* sound and the nose. Some of the words that describe attitudes are associated with facial expressions that involve "wrinkling the nose at" or "looking down the nose at."

An Annotated Bibliographical Note

For those who would like further information about the evolution of English, the essay "Language, Culture and the American Heritage" by Lee Pederson in *The American Heritage Dictionary* (Boston: Houghton Mifflin, 1982) and the essay "Indo-European and the Indo-Europeans" by Calvert Watkins in *The American Heritage Dictionary of Indo-European Roots* (Boston: Houghton Mifflin, 1985) provide excellent summaries of scholarship in the field, as does the essay "The Indo-European Origin of English" by Calvert Watkins in the 1969 edition of *The American Heritage Dictionary*. Two fine books on the subject are *Our Marvelous Native Tongue: The Life and Times of the English Language* by Robert Claiborne (New York: Times Books, 1983) and *The Story of English* by Robert McCrum, William Cran, and Robert MacNeil (New York: Viking, 1986). Both books are written with wit and grace and an appreciation both for the treasures of the past buried in the language and for the delights of the newly coined words that constantly enrich the language. *Our Marvelous Native Tongue* follows a straightforward chronology, whereas *The Story of English*, a companion to a PBS television series, pays particular attention to the development of English around the world, ranging from Scotland and Ireland to Australia, Jamaica, West Africa, and India, as well as the United States. Both books provide good and provocative discussions of black English. The two books are complementary.

Classic books in the field are Albert Baugh's *A History of the English Language* (New York: Appleton-Century Crofts, 1957); Otto Jesperson's *Growth and Structure of the English Language* (New York: The Free Press, 1968); and Thomas Pyle's *The Origins and Development of the English Language* (New York: Harcourt, Brace & World, 1964). Two highly readable overviews of the subject, written for teachers and students, are J.N. Hook's *The Story of British English* (Oakland, N.J.: Scott, Foresman, 1974) and Marshall Brown's *Language: The Origins of English* (Columbus, Ohio: Charles E. Merrill Publishing Co., 1971). Unfortunately these books are out of print, but you may be able to find them in the library. Two gracefully written books that give particular attention to the way historical experience is reflected in etymology are Logan Pearsall Smith's *The English Language* (New York: Henry Holt and Company, 1912) and Owen Barfield's *History in English Words* (first published in 1925 and reprinted by Lindisfarne Press, Great Barrington, Massachusetts, 1985). *The English Language* has been reprinted only in a library edition, though it can be special-ordered through bookstores. Another book by Robert Claiborne, *The Roots of English: A Reader's Handbook of Word Origins* (New York: Times Books, 1989) discusses word families revealed by Indo-European roots.

Books that cover grammar, phonology, and social aspects of English, as well as its history, are *The Gift of Language* by Margaret Schlauch (New York: Dover, 1955) and *Origins of the English Language: A Social and Linguistic History* by Joseph Williams (New York: Macmillan, 1975). Peter Farb's *Word Play: What Happens When People Talk* (New York: Knopf, 1973) pays particular attention to how social rules shape the way we speak—and how these rules differ in different cultures.

A book that stands in a class by itself is *1066: The Year of the Conquest* by David Howarth (New York: Viking, 1977). Howarth, a wonderful storyteller, describes the Norman Conquest in vivid detail, taking us intimately into the lives of the English and the Normans, as well as the Norsemen, whose attack in northern Britain was a proximate cause of King Harold's defeat by the Normans at the Battle of Hastings on the southern coast. Since all of these peoples were important to the development of English, the book can be read as more than just a tale of battle.

For those interested in exploring American popular speech and its role in the historical development of English, we recommend (in addition to *Our Marvelous Native Tongue* and *The Story of English*) the lively and irreverent *American Tongue and Cheek* by Jim Quinn (New York: Pantheon Books, 1980) as well as H.L. Mencken's classic work in a similarly irreverent vein, *The American Language* (New York: Alfred A. Knopf, 1937). Mencken's book and its Supplements I and II were abridged and updated by Reven McDavid in 1963. *Our Own Words* (New York: Alfred A. Knopf, 1974) by Mary Helen Dohan explores the interplay of history and language as it is reflected in the development of American vocabulary. *Chin Music, Tall Talk and Other Talk* (New York: J.B. Lippincott, 1979) reports on American folk speech collected by Alvin Schwartz, and *Down in the Holler: A Gallery of Ozark Folk-Speech* by Vance

Randolph and George P. Wilson (Norman, Oklahoma: Oklahoma University Press, 1953) is a classic. *American Talk: The Words and Ways of American Dialects* by Robert Hendrickson (New York: Viking, 1986) provides an appreciative look at the life and origins of American regional speech, and *A Dictionary of American Idioms*, edited by Adam Makka (New York: Barron's, 1987), is a treasure trove of informal American speech. The *Dictionary of American Regional English,* edited by Frederic G. Cassidy (Cambridge, Massachusetts: Harvard University Press), is an ambitious and continuing survey of American folk and regional speech. Volume I, which includes the Introduction and entries under A-C, was published in 1985. The introductory essays provide a good overview of American regional speech. The research for the *Dictionary* is being done by the American Dialect Society at the University of Wisconsin in Madison, and researchers are very kind about answering written inquiries.

We highly recommend Geneva Smitherman's *Talkin and Testifyin* (Boston: Houghton Mifflin, 1975), which both analyzes and reflects the vitality of black vernacular English. In the course of her wide-ranging analysis of black speech, she explores both the influence of African languages and the influence of African oral tradition. Edith Folb's *runnin down some lines* (Cambridge, Massachusetts: Harvard University Press, 1980) pays homage to the linguistic creativity of African-American teenagers as exemplified by the language of young people in the Watts and South Central area of Los   Angeles. Lawrence Levine's *Black Culture and Black Consciousness* (New York: Oxford University Press, 1977) and Thomas Kochman's *Black and White Styles in Conflict* (Chicago: University of Chicago Press, 1981) are excellent books that give special emphasis to the creativity of African-American cultural tradition.

Rudolph Arnheim looks at the way language is grounded in experience from a slightly different perspective—that of a philosopher of the arts. Against a background of exploring the role of perception and abstraction in the arts and in all thought, he observes that "the histories of languages show that words which do not seem now to refer to direct perceptual experience did so originally." His observations on language are found in the chapter "Words in Their Place" in his *Visual Thinking* (London: Faber and Faber Ltd., 1969). In *Functions of Language in the Classroom* (New York: Teachers College Press, 1972), edited by Courtney Cazden, Vera John, and Dell Hymes, Eleanor

Leacock's "Abstract Versus Concrete Speech: A False Dichotomy" describes the ways in which both popular and erudite language are metaphorical. She analyzes the abstract thinking reflected in both and considers the implications of this analysis for those who teach. *Metaphors We Live By* by George Lakoff and Mark Johnson (Chicago: University of Chicago Press, 1980) looks at how metaphor operates as a fundamental vehicle of thought, both shaping and expressing our view of the world. Mark Johnson's *The Body in the Mind: The Bodily Basis of Meaning, Imagination, and Reason* (Chicago: University of Chicago Press, 1987) expands on the work of *Metaphors We Live By*.

For a discussion of dictionaries we have used in exploring word histories, see the "Sources and Materials" section of the "Introduction" and the "Developing Your Own Word Families" section of the "Using Origins" chapter.

For those interested in student activities that bear specifically on the history of English, Good Apple Press (Box 299, Carthage, IL 62321) publishes two workbooks for students in grades 4-8: *What's in a Word: Word History Activity Sheets* by David Zaslow and *Slanguage: Activities and Ideas on the History and Nature of Language* by John Artman.

Appendix

The Words Project

Origins is at the center of a larger venture, the Words Project. Below are descriptions of various Words Project experiments, along with opportunities for you to take part.

Using *Origins* as a Base for a Literacy Program

We used the materials of *Origins* as a base for a literacy program when we ran a pilot program for the Job Corps for twelve students, ages 19 to 21, who were reading at second- and third-grade levels. Celia Alvaraz, a linguist who now teaches at Columbia University, worked in partnership with me to plan and run the program.

We devised a weekly cycle of activities that included introducing a word family, generating and decoding other words based on spelling patterns of words in the family, playing card games to review and study these word groups and words of the families, and reading poetry (mostly by African-American poets, since the students were African-American) that used the imagery of the family. Finally, drawing on all the vocabulary that had become familiar during the week, students did their own writing. The cycle of the following week began as students read each other's writing, which we had typed up and copied over the weekend.

Despite initial resistance, the students got genuinely involved with the material. Exploring items of their own speech seized their attention and gave them a sense of connection with those who had coined the vocabulary of the word families. We started with the BHEL family. *Bold* vaulted them into competitive posing, and laughter and play-acting replaced their indifference. The playful spirit carried over into the more mundane activity of decoding words that shared spelling patterns with words of the family, and was reinforced by reviewing the patterns through card games, which students infused with their own sense of drama and panache. The poetry (such as Langston Hughes' "The Negro Speaks of Rivers") evoked a strong sense of connection; virtually every student wanted to struggle through what for them was the challenging vocabulary—which we reviewed ahead of time—to do his or her own reading of the poem. At every turn we praised success, helped out where needed, and ignored errors. Students picked up on our attitude and played by the ground rules of respecting and not criticizing each other—an attitude especially important when it came to their own writing. We presented writing as an opportunity, provided any help requested, and expressed confidence in their abilities. If a student simply copied a few lines of the poem—which was posted on the wall along with all the other vocabulary of the week—we said, "That's great. Can you add a few lines of your own?" Each week we added new vocabulary without taking down the old, so that students gradually became surrounded by a huge quantity of familiar vocabulary. Though students' first attempts were extremely rudimentary, we typed them all (correcting spelling but leaving the grammar natural to students' own speech), copied them, and invited students to read their own writing aloud for each other. The typed copies were greeted with "This looks like re*al* writing." Every student wanted to read—and they all continued to share their work each week as their efforts were greeted with appreciation.

The program lasted five weeks, and subsequent funding cuts eliminated any opportunity to try a longer program. In five weeks there were no significant changes in test results. We saw many significant changes in the students, however, which we felt would translate into test results over a longer span. One student, whose first efforts at writing produced "The ball is on the hill," wrote a story half a page long during the last week of the program—for him a real triumph. We saw a young woman who had produced a few modest and uninspired lines each week suddenly blossom into writing a jazz poem, which she read aloud with verve and rhythm. Students were playful with the words of the families, tossing them back and forth as they chatted around the edges of the class, and they made steady progress in mastering increasing numbers of words for spelling tests. Most important, they became serious about their own work, taking pride in what they produced. Their regular reading teacher, whose class they continued to attend, reported that the students' motivation and commitment to learning increased markedly in her class. We would be happy to send a copy of our full report on the project to anyone who is interested. Write to us at: The Words Project, 6404 Ridge Drive, Brookmont, MD 20816.

Inventing Stone Age Languages

At the Sidwell Friends School in Washington, D.C., Priscilla Alfandre has used *Origins* as a resource for having her third- and fourth-grade students invent their own primitive languages in conjunction with studying Neanderthal people. The challenge of giving a voice and a vocabulary to these ancient ancestors excited students and prompted them to think clearly and precisely about the experiences of Stone Age hunters and gatherers. Priscilla responded to the excitement by carrying the project through to a highly elaborated conclusion. After initial brainstorming as a group, students were divided into three "tribes," and each tribe invented and recorded the basic nouns and verbs they would need for everyday activities and communication. Each group had an adult working with it. In preparation for writing dialogues and stories in their tribal languages, students then went on to devise other words that were still needed. This was difficult and challenging work, requiring a clear understanding of language and history, an understanding Priscilla helped engender as she guided her students. Her vivid account tells how she and her students progressed toward making dictionaries and writing stories and a Neanderthal burial ceremony in their invented languages. We will be glad to send you a copy of her report.

Using *Origins* in French Class

At the Capitol Hill Day School in Washington, D.C., Ann Craig, a French teacher, has used the history of English as a resource for having seventh and eighth graders introduce fifth and sixth graders to French. Starting with the announcement, "This story is going to tell you what a difference was made in the English language by the victory of William the Conqueror," her seventh and eighth graders staged a replay of the Norman Conquest for their fifth/sixth grade audience. The actors had researched and developed the drama themselves. At the end of the play, an announcer brought out a list of French words that had almost identical counterparts in English, and the fifth and sixth graders enthusiastically identified the English counterparts. After this lively (and often humorous) introduction, the fifth/sixth grade classroom teacher continued to point out connections between French and English vocabulary as she prepared students for beginning a formal study of French. We will be glad to send you a report on this project.

Exploring Cross-Cultural Metaphors

Exploring cross-cultural metaphors is relatively new territory for us. So far, we have had time for initial research (conducted through interviews with native speakers), but not enough time for collecting an abundance of examples. We are continuing the research. We would be interested in hearing about work you have done with students in this area. For an update on our research and for information about participating, write to us.

A Final Word

Origins is in a state of continual evolution. Every time we assimilate new ideas and sketch new possibilities for using the material, we begin to see further possiblities for its use. We are interested to know how you are using the material and what questions and ideas you might have. We have done preliminary work on a future volume that would include the DRAGH- (to pull), GENE- (to give birth), PED- (foot), SED- (to sit), SKER- (to cut), and STA- (to stand) families listed in the "Additional Word Families Based on Indo-European Roots" section of the "Linguistic Background" chapter. In that future volume we would like to focus on the multitude of metaphors that spring from certain basic images— in the form of Latin words, in the form of Germanic words and phrases, and in metaphors drawn from other languages around the world. For example, there are many words and phrases built on the Germanic word for *stand* as well as many words (both Latinate and Germanic) built on the root STA (to stand). Are there also metaphors based on images of *standing* in languages wholly unrelated to English? Seems likely. We would like to explore such metaphors and imagery in poetry as well as in individual words, and we hope to draw the poetry from as many languages and cultures as possible. We would like to explore further the stylistic choices created by the many synonymous pairings of Latinate words and Germanic words or phrases that are found in English.

The volume would be geared toward junior high and high school levels and designed to be used as a resource in teaching literature and writing.

We would be interested in any suggestions, questions, samples of poetry, etc. that you might have. Write us at:

The Words Project
6404 Ridge Drive
Brookmont, MD 20816.

(Sound cousins)